We Laughed at her Funeral

Bits of Wit and Wisdom from Real Life

CAROL THORNBURG GRIMES

BOOKSIDE Press

Copyright © 2024 by Carol Thornburg Grimes

ISBN: 978-1-77883-304-5 (Paperback)

All rights reserved. No part of this publication may be reproduced, distributed, or transmitted in any form or by any means, including photocopying, recording, or other electronic or mechanical methods, without the prior written permission of the publisher, except in the case of brief quotations embodied in critical reviews and other noncommercial uses permitted by copyright law.

The views expressed in this book are solely those of the author and do not necessarily reflect the views of the publisher, and the publisher hereby disclaims any responsibility for them. Some names and identifying details in this book have been changed to protect the privacy of individuals.

BookSide Press
877-741-8091
www.booksidepress.com
orders@booksidepress.com

Contents

Introduction vii
Dedication ix
Acknowledgements x

Part One
    Mother Stories: A New View 1
    Meet My Mother 3
    The Good Treasure 6
    The Mix Up 8
    Mother's Little Helpers 11
    The Great Escape 12
    Fishes and Dishes 15
    A Family Resemblance 17
    Pride Goeth Before A Slip 20
    Keepsake Box 24
    It's Here Somewhere 26
    Changing Places 28
    And the Winner Is... 31
    Move Along... 35
    The Gift of Love 36

Part Two
    My Heart Has A Green Thumb 41
    Spider In My Flower Pot 42
    The Laughin' Place 43
    Giant Oaks and Little Sins 47
    Bloom Where You Are 50
    The Importance of Mud Pies 53

Resurrection 56
Mine To Keep 58
Tender Shoots 59
My Friendship Garden.. 62

Part Three
What Happens When I Stop, Look, and Listen 66
Lest I Forget 67
Squeeze of A Lifetime 70
The Lion In the Log 73
Measuring Up 76
Maze of Faith.. 80
Everyday A New Beginning 83
Affluence 86
Road To Success.. 89
Was My Prayer Answered? 92
The Fabric of Faith 96
Stop, Look, and Listen... 99
Spiritual Computerish 103
Love: The Real Thing 106
Does It Matter?... 109
A Heavenly View 112
For God So Loved the World.................................... 115
It's Just A Little Thing.. 121
My Clock Will Not Run Backwards 124
Only One Thing Is Needed 128
The Gift of Giving.. 132

Part Four
Poetry, Prayers, and Pondering................................. 137
Envy the Season's Change 138
Love Knot.. 141
A Marriage Prayer... 142
Big Hands and Little Hands 143
A Day Too Late... 145
The Measure of A Man.. 147

As Others See Me	149
To Our Grandparents	150
Invocation for Missions	151
Life In Any Lane	153
When	154
Why	155
Getting At the Truth	156
Yesterday's Sandcastles	157
Prayer Without Words	160
Are You Listening???	164
When I Grow Up	168
Where Have the Heroes Gone?	172

Part Five

Letters Shared	176
A Letter... Finally Written	177
Sadness	180
About That Question	181
Two Roads To the Same Place	185
Thank You Note	187
Keep Your Heart	188
Heart of A Shepherd	190
A Hard Choice	192
My Bad!	194
It Is Enough	196
The Real Christmas	197
In Search of Christmas Lost	198
No Room In the Inn	201
Christmas Light	203
The View From Old	206

Introduction

As long as I can remember, I've been doing the same things–trying to grow things and trying to express with words my belief in God. Collecting ideas to write about has been easy, but learning the necessary skills has not. God knew I needed help. He made me wait a long time, and all the while He tutored me. Some of the lessons have been difficult, while others were wonderful experiences. First, I had to learn the rules; read and write, read and write, over and over. Then I had to learn to share what I instinctively believed. Many years of teaching Sunday School provided that opportunity. I started by teaching little ones, who are uncritical and accepting. From them I gained a measure of self-confidence. Next were young people. They questioned my every idea, but their scrutiny taught me to research facts. Then my turn came to teach adults who were older and wiser in both knowledge and experience. It was from them I learned humility and respect for the hard-earned opinions of others. Finally, the Lord provided an opportunity for me to write a short monthly column for our church newsletter, *the Diligent*. For that assignment, I had to practice and produce.

All the while, God exposed me daily to situations and people with something to teach me. Just as often He interfered with plans of my own that would have led me astray. In the process I earned a college degree, acquired a job which exposed me to countless people I would never have known, and refined my writing skills.

God instilled in me the desire to write. He enhanced my skills, provided the subject matter, and He expects me to succeed. I must try.

Dedication

This collection is for my family and friends who have encouraged me to gather my "closet writing" into a book. I would never have had the confidence to do so otherwise. *You* know who you are. Thank you.

Acknowledgements

Between graduate school classes and her job at the Children's Museum in Indianapolis, our granddaughter Alyssa Porter, did the graphics for the book. Thank you, Lyss, for the sketches and for keeping our work a secret. Our son, Mike, has edited for me since the beginning, one article at a time, before being sent to the *the Diligent*. He has an eagle's eye and is both objective and encouraging. Thank you, Mike. Without the technical assistance of my daughter-in-law, Tami, this book would still be lost in my computer. Thank you, Tami, for answering the midnight calls.

Years ago, a college professor, whose name I no longer remember, required that the class keep a daily notebook with observations of people, places, and things. Because that notebook was going to count for half of my semester grade, I applied myself. Once I learned to stop, look, and listen, every one of my senses woke up. People came into focus, nature became even more alive, and my mind thought it was a sponge. Thank you, Professor, for opening my eyes. Stored in my mind and in my notebooks is a library of quotes, stories, and information that made an impression worth remembering. If I have quoted you without permission or acknowledgement, please believe that I now regret not having kept better documentation. Please consider yourself thanked sincerely.

Part One

Mother Stories: A New View

My mother was definitely unique. She was a non-conformist a long time before it was *in* to be *far out*. I loved her dearly, but somewhat privately. Publicly she very often embarrassed me.

For too many years, I focused my attention on reforming my mother instead of appreciating her. How foolish I was. I learned late what others knew all the time; what my mother lacked in conformity, she more than made up for with congeniality. Mother handled it very well though. I think she always knew I would smarten up. That revelation came when I realized how often I quoted her and how many humorous and heart-warming stories I told about her idiosyncrasies.

Mother didn't preach or lecture to us, but she never missed an opportunity to teach us right from wrong with an object lesson and those we remember to this day. We didn't have any hard and fast rules, but with her honor system we didn't need them. I never thought of Mother as religious, but as good. She told people we were Methodists, even though we rarely went to church, but I always knew ours was a Christian family.

Now that my vision has cleared, I regret not having enjoyed my mother more.

However, knowing how readily she laughed at herself and how much she enjoyed publicity, I'm sure that sharing these stories with others could very well make her the happiest woman in heaven.

Meet My Mother

My mother was a very pretty lady. When she was fixed up, she really turned heads. Actually, she always turned heads because when she wasn't fixed up she was a mess. No matter what length her dress was, her slip was longer. I gave up trying to adjust the straps because they were always knotted and usually dangling near her elbow from her sleeve. As long as there were enough buttons left to keep her garment on she never bothered to replace one, even if it meant the remaining ones sometimes had to reach up or down to a neighboring buttonhole to close the gap.

Mother always said she wasn't very good with hair. I never knew for sure if that were true or an excuse for hers. In those days we pin-curled our hair and she could never find enough bobby pins at one time to do it right, so she half did it. Literally. I didn't mind it so much when she did up the front and left the back loose, but when she did up the back and left the front loose, I just couldn't look–and she laughed at me.

My meticulous grandmother was more than a little bothered by this carelessness on Mother's part, and I never doubted Grandma when she told me it was a trait Mother got from her father. Grandma never used any bad language except for one word, and she always used that one in the same statement to my mother. "Mildred," she would say, "you're as bad as your father. He would go to town with shit on him if I would let him." But I don't think that even then Grandma ever used the word to be vulgar, just descriptive. Grandpa was a farmer.

Mother didn't spend a lot of time shopping for clothes. When she did find something she liked, she rarely tried it on. If I told her I thought it was too big, she would tell me that she was sure it would fit because the color was just right. I remember when I finally got up the nerve to ask for my first bra. Actually, I didn't need one at all, but I was sixteen and I wanted it to hang over the locker door in gym class like everyone else. She was very matter-of-fact about it and brought me one home the same day. I will never forget how I felt when my brother held up what must have been at least an extra large and said, "Mother, have you ever looked at her?" Unfortunately, I never did grow into that bra, but it did get me some attention in the locker room. I wonder now if she knew all the time what she was doing.

I made more excuses to my friends for my mother's appearance than I did for my father's drinking. After all, they had all seen someone under the influence, but never anyone who would wear shoes that didn't match. Strangely enough they thought I was lucky. They all had ordinary moms.

Mother never changed. At her funeral I heard her friends talking about "how nice she looked." Then I heard someone in the group whisper to another that she thought Mother would look more natural if her dress were

Meet My Mother

on wrong-side-out. Others around smiled and nodded in agreement. They remembered what fun they all had the day Mother went to church that way, and her most of all.

Listening to that group of white-haired ladies exchange favorite stories about her, I began to realize just how special she really was. I was sure that no ordinary mother ever had so many friends laughing at her funeral.

The Good Treasure

My mother lived in many different places during her life. She used to tell me two of the disadvantages of frequently moving were losing things and leaving behind things she would have liked to take. The loss that mattered most to her was her wedding dishes. What she hated to leave behind most of all were her flowers. Mother planted flowers everywhere she ever lived even if she knew it was going to be a short stay. When she had to leave that place she always dug up a few to take along. A few more that is, than the number Dad said was the absolute limit.

When Mother made her final move to a home where nothing is ever lost and where the flowers are perpetual, I moved those she left behind to my house. I knew that some of those flowers had lived in a lot more places than I had. The amaryllis, for example, had really been around, and I'm sure Mother knew where each one originated. I only knew where they wound up–in a cardboard box beside my back step. Mother would have put those bulbs in the ground before she put sheets on the bed, but I spent considerable time planning. While I was deciding where to plant them, winter came and went and the amaryllis stayed in the box.

One morning in mid-spring, I stepped out the back door and was greeted by a lovely surprise. It was an

The Good Treasure

assortment of red and pink and white amaryllis blooms arranged in a weather beaten cardboard box with brown foliage hanging over the edges. Never had I seen a more beautiful bouquet. Despite total neglect, those flowers were blooming where they were. I knew that they were able to do so only because everything essential had been stored inside the bulbs.

My mother's flowers reminded me of something she used to tell me when, as a young self-conscious girl, I didn't have all I thought I needed to be like my friends. "Pretty comes from within," she would say, "and no matter what you do to the outside, what you are on the inside will always show through." I know now that my mother was paraphrasing Him who said, "*A good man out of the good treasure of his heart bringeth forth good things. . .*" (*Matthew 12:35*).

The day the amaryllis bloomed in the cardboard box may have been the first time I really thought about my heart's treasury, but it won't be the last.

The Mix Up

My mother had one sister, but nothing about the two of them would ever have given a clue that they were in any way related. My aunt was very neat about her personal appearance as well as her house. She was also organized. She shopped on the same day each week, washed on the same day, and even folded up the ironing board sometimes. She always knew everything that was going on at her house and could keep track of the one week of the month for a trip to the lake that was agreeable to all three females in the family.

I loved it at my aunt's house, especially at mealtime. Her family all sat down at the table at one time and in the same chair each night regardless of who got there first. There was one drawback though; they had to eat what she prepared. My mother fixed special orders.

I thought my aunt was amazing. She put things in the same place more than once and knew where her purse was at all times. Of course, that was a disadvantage for my cousins; they couldn't earn money finding it for her like my brothers and I could. Every time Mother lost her purse she gave one of us a quarter to find it, and she lost it every time she put it down. My brother is the only person I know who paid his college tuition in quarters. One of the first things my children learned about their grandmother was that it paid to remember where she put her keys.

The Mix Up

Come to think of it, that was another advantage we had. Our mother could drive a car and wasn't afraid of anything, so we got to go lots of places. Since she always saved the housework for another day, we went often.

My aunt had two daughters. One was like her. The other poor thing was just like my mother, and the grownups in the family always treated her as if fate had dealt her a losing hand. I guess she really was like Mother though, because despite all the trouble she got into she was always happy. She didn't even seem to mind when people mixed us up and thought she belonged to my mother. I couldn't understand that because I was embarrassed when they thought I belonged to Mother, and I did. My aunt and I had some common traits, too. Neither of us ever suspected that my mother and my cousin sometimes sneaked a smoke together in the orange grove behind the house.

I was sometimes envious of my cousins. They had all kinds of things that we didn't: chores, curfews, study hours, and even rules. All we ever had was an honor system. My cousins could get around their regulations sometimes, but Mother's guilt trap was foolproof. It was simply impossible to lie to a mother who believed everything you told her. At least it was for me. My brothers were a little more successful. As if the honor system were not enough, she thought we were perfect. Despite their attempts, my brothers never changed her mind about that.

My cousins took piano lessons. They practiced at predetermined times and my aunt listened while they did. I took piano lessons, too. I practiced when I wanted to and what I didn't remember I made up. I thought I was doing very well until my aunt came over to listen to me practice. After that I didn't take piano lessons anymore, but I liked the elocution lessons better anyway. There are those, however, who think Mother made a mistake when she encouraged that "talent."

Time and miles came between my cousins and me and for too many years we didn't see one another at all. But Mother took care of that. We did what we somehow always manage to do for the dead, but find so difficult to do for the living. We got together. How surprised I was to find out that my cousins had envied me my unconventional mother. The stories we shared about her that day were wonderful fun despite the occasion, and I couldn't even feel guilty about laughing because I knew that nothing would have pleased Mother more.

Mother's Little Helpers

There were many things that Mother never learned to do, but nothing she could not get done. For instance, she didn't sew at all, but she made me a beautiful quilt.

"I made this one for you, and I think it's my prettiest one yet," Mother said. "Sarah cut the pieces because she has all the newest gadgets. She tried to show me how to use them, but I have trouble getting them all the same and she doesn't have much patience with me. She was so proud of the way they turned out.

"Edna pieced them together. She's the only one that can make stitches so tiny. She is a widow and has so much time on her hands that I thought it would be good for her to have something to keep her busy. I picked a backing I knew you would like and tried to help Ruth tack it all together, but she is such a perfectionist she has to do everything herself.

"We quilted it at the last Circle meeting, but I didn't get to go. They really miss me when I'm not there. Everyone just loves this one. I could've sold it easily, but I wouldn't, not for any amount because I made it especially for you."

Then in a low voice behind her hand she said, "My friends think I can do anything."

So do I, Mother. So do I.

The Great Escape

I had a dog once who could play dead, but that was no trick at all compared to the way my mother could play dumb. I know it was an act she perfected, because no one really dumb could have done it so well. I referred to it as her Houdini routine because combined with her talent for creating confusion it could get her out of anything. She was so good at it in fact, it even worked on me and I knew better. However, I always thought police officers were her specialty.

In Mother's lifetime she probably talked personally to every patrolman assigned to traffic, but at 75 she could still boast of a perfect driving record. Never once did she get a ticket–or should I say, accept a ticket. I remember the time she parked her car outside a large shopping area and left it in gear. When she came back and discovered it gone she immediately found a policeman and reported it stolen. As it happened, he was looking for the owner of a car that had rolled through the parking lot, across a four-lane highway, and into a parking space in a fast food restaurant. The lost were found.

Everything would have been fine if it had ended there. Instead, the naïve police officer attempted to give her a ticket. Why? She couldn't imagine. She hadn't driven it there, it hadn't hit a thing, and it was parked properly. Since she couldn't get the young man to understand his

The Great Escape

error, she welcomed his suggestion that she explain it to the judge. My dad pleaded with her to pay the fine, but she believed she was right and went to court to prove it. The judge needed a good lawyer. He lost the case, and the poor harmless victim of circumstances came away with only a few pointers for parking on a hill. The judge retired. After suffering through another of her, *"See, what I told you?"* sessions, Dad vowed once more to never again interfere.

Mother was innately honest and optimistic, and therefore not bothered a lot about details like where to keep her driver's license. She knew she had one, knew it was all in good order, and that the chances of her needing it were highly unlikely. One day when she was stopped for a routine license check it appeared that her luck had run out. As it turned out, the police officers' luck had run out. Unruffled, she explained to him in great detail, while rummaging through her purse, that she definitely had it somewhere. What she didn't tell him was that "somewhere" encompassed her entire belongings. He allowed her to continue looking while he checked cars behind her. When he returned, she showed him our school pictures since first grade, and her grandchildren's pictures since first grade. While I slowly slithered out of sight under the seat, he motioned for the cars lined up behind us to go around, and she smiled sweetly and emptied her purse in her lap. On his third trip back, which was getting to be a hefty hike by now, she pulled out the yard-long, accordion-pleated, plastic cardholder, and started removing one item at a time. It was then that he decided to trust her.

Mother could adapt the Houdini routine to almost every situation. She never lost an argument, because she never finished one that wasn't going well. Since she believed only what she chose to believe, Mother rarely got her feelings hurt and almost never took criticism seriously. The way she handled gossip was to so confuse the facts that no one could ever repeat it. I thought she told wonderful stories because they were different every time, and the talent she had for getting other people to do things for her would have made Tom Sawyer hang his head in shame.

I remember now that Mother frequently warned me about getting too smart for my own good, but I wasn't even smart enough to know what she was telling me.

Fishes and Dishes

Everyone who ever ate Mother's cooking thought she was a wonderful cook. I learned as many of her secrets as I could, but there is one that is still a mystery. She and that little boy with the loaves and fishes were the only two people I ever heard of who could feed so many with so little.

I think Mother somehow equated love with food because she always wanted to feed people. It didn't matter who came or how unexpected they were, she insisted that they stay and eat; even when it looked like there wasn't enough for us, but there always was. Of course, she never ate anything herself on those occasions because she was busy waiting on everyone. I guess that association between food and love rubbed off on me at an early age because one of her favorite stories was about the time she was entertaining in the living room and I sneaked off to the kitchen and fixed a bowl of cereal for each of her friends.

Mother really was a picky eater. I know she didn't like steak because she only bought enough for the rest of us. We had to take turns getting the wishbone of the chicken, and she never ate any of the white meat unless there happened to be a wing left when everyone had finished. I was a mother myself before I realized that mothers don't really prefer the heels of bread, broken cookies, and burned toast.

I tried to avoid washing dishes at my mother's house

unless I had a lot of time because she always picked that time to clean out the refrigerator, and there were often skillets in the oven she had saved to wash later.

For a while, Mother managed the cafeteria in a small elementary school. It wasn't long before she knew all the children by name and their likes and dislikes. There were always decorated cakes on special days and an extra cookie on your plate if it was your birthday. And best of all, it was okay if you didn't clean your plate.

While I didn't think at the time that I would ever want to be like her, I always knew I wanted to cook like her. Her pies were almost revered, and although I have the recipes, they didn't come with her magic touch. My cousin was visiting recently and I fixed homemade pancakes for his breakfast. "These are the second best pancakes I've ever eaten," he said, and I took it as the supreme compliment.

A Family Resemblance

When I was growing up my mother didn't worry a lot about appearances. She never could manage to part my hair straight and it didn't bother her if my slip happened to be a little longer than my dress. It did matter a great deal though, how I behaved. She made a point of reminding me that my behavior was a direct reflection on her. That didn't make a bit of sense to me until I had children of my own. That is when I learned that *a reflection on her* meant *a likeness to her.* It meant being polite, respectful, honest, obedient, helpful, and all the other things that she was and wanted me to be. It wasn't easy, and I am sure that I often did her injustice. Today people who never knew my mother see only what I display and I want that always to be a true reflection.

I think that at one time or another most people say things like, "The baby looks just like his daddy," "She doesn't look a bit like her sister," or "You wouldn't know they were related by the way they behave." On and on it goes, judging by appearances. Outward appearance is usually the first and most obvious reflection we make. Take me for instance; I shower, dust, and spray. Then I moisturize and texturize, and put on camouflage. I suck it in, pull it up, push it out, and then I coordinate and decorate, in hopes that others will appreciate. After all of that, nothing has changed but the looks of me, and that is the problem with outward appearance. Sometimes it even fools us into believing that we are something we aren't. That is when my mother would have told me, "pretty is as pretty does," and that under my pretty clothes I was still naked.

Our words more accurately reflect our hearts. The scriptures tell us that it is from the abundance of the heart that the mouth speaks. Mother's paraphrase would have been, "Your conversation is your advertisement." Our talk may be misleading, but our hearts speak clearly. A kind heart doesn't say spiteful things. A compassionate heart doesn't repeat gossip. A forgiving heart doesn't condemn. A generous heart doesn't degrade. A grateful heart gives praise. A caring heart gives encouragement. A wise heart gives healing words. A loving heart gives acceptance. A pure heart speaks truthfully. The heart of a friend keeps confidences.

The truest reflection isn't our appearance or our words, but our deeds. A long time before my mother told me that actions speak louder than words, the scripture said, *"Wherefore by their fruits you shall know them" (Matthew 7:20).*

> *"Who is wise and understanding among you? Let him show it by his good life, by deeds done in the humility that comes from wisdom" (James 3:13, NIV).*

There are many scriptures that describe the way we should love others and do good; the way we should show a likeness to our Heavenly Father.

All around us in our community, our workplaces, our homes, and among our families and friends are those who know nothing about our God except what we, His children, are reflecting. Do you ever wonder what you are telling them?

Pride Goeth Before A Slip

When we were growing up we didn't have a lot of rules at our house. As a matter of fact, I think our mother told us the day we were born about right and wrong, and that done never expected to have to mention it again. She did, however, expect us forever after to know the difference. When we messed up, she countered with an object lesson and we were the objects. It was a very effective tactic. Who wants their mother telling the same story about them for the next forty years? There were a few things though, that Mother felt strongly enough about to emphasize. One of those was vanity and a particular slipup I made in that area became one of her favorite stories.

The vanity lectures always started out the same. "Nice girls don't. . ." The one I remember best was, "Nice girls don't look at themselves in store windows." I knew that one well and was usually quite successful in avoiding such blatant egotism. But one day, despite my good training and self-discipline, I yielded to temptation. It happened about the time that knee-high, real leather boots were going out of style, and I had just gotten in-style enough to buy a pair. To go with them I had put together a simply marvelous outfit, with a skirt split high in the front and in the back, a turtleneck sweater, a waist-clenching belt, and all the accessories I could wear and remain upright. Where I got

Pride Goeth Before A Slip

the nerve to go out in public in such uncharacteristic garb I still don't know; but with a rare assurance that I finally had it all together, I ventured downtown.

When I found myself alone in front of a row of glass-fronted stores, I absolutely could not resist stealing a glance. When I did, what I saw wasn't at all what I expected. Instead, there I was in my short, sleek skirt with the split in the front and the split in the back, and my slip down around my real leather boots. To make matters worse, I heard a voice ask, "Do you have a problem, Carol?" Standing behind me was my neighbor. I was profoundly embarrassed about my downed slip, but that could not compare with how I felt about being caught looking at myself in the store window. When word of it got back to Mother, it moved to the top of her list. In my ears rang a familiar scripture.

"Pride goeth before destruction and a haughty spirit before a fall" (Proverbs 16:12, NIV).

If Mother sometimes appeared less than humble about her family, it was a necessary sacrifice she made for our good. She knew even back then about the importance of a good self-image, except she called it "pride in yourself." That kind of pride, you understand, was good, and quite a different thing than vanity. Even though it was hard to believe all the reassuring things Mother told me, it was a great comfort to hear her say that "red-faced" really meant natural beauty, and that "skinny" meant I would grow up to be just right and the well-proportioned girls I envied would probably be fat. She explained that "no dates" was a sign that the boys respected me and not to worry because those popular girls were not the ones they married anyway.

It was no secret that Mother was proud of her children. I was only about five years old when I realized that other mothers didn't introduce their little girls saying, "This is my daughter, isn't she pretty?" If there was a more embarrassing way of presenting me, Mother never thought of it, because as long as she lived she did the same thing. I cringed every time, afraid of what she might say next if someone dared to answer her honestly. At least as often as she bragged on me though, she reminded me how I looked was none of my own doing and gave me no cause to feel proud, but what kind of person I was depended entirely on me.

Even the way Mother introduced herself was a spin-off of her pride in us. Because my brothers had acquired a modest amount of success in the town where we lived, simply mentioning them by their first name was all she ever felt necessary. If the other person didn't immediately make the connection, she forgave and enlightened them.

Despite her constant praise, Mother expected us to remain humble. The public acclaim was her privilege exclusively. When a friend of hers (whom I scarcely knew) reported to her that I had snubbed her husband (whom I knew not at all), Mother called me in for a gentle head shrinking. After that everyone thought I was very friendly. Unfortunately, the old gentleman died a short time later and I can't help hoping he didn't die of a broken heart.

Pride Goeth Before A Slip

There were other "nice girls" guidelines as well. Nice girls never called boys on the telephone, or kissed on a first date. Nice girls didn't swear or use vulgar language, and promptly blushed in response to any they overheard. Nice girls didn't wear a lot of makeup and never showed a hint a cleavage, if one were fortunate enough to have any. Definite dress codes, even if unwritten, set nice girls apart.

Most of that was no problem at all for me because I wanted to please my mother. I wanted her to be proud of me as long as she lived. Looking back, I believe her expectations for each of us were everyday examples of what she thought would please God. In return, any honor that came to one of her children, Mother wore like a badge. Now it is our turn to be proud. Countless, ongoing expressions of love and admiration for our mother have become a source of pride to us, and our treasured trophies.

"For whoever exalts himself will be humbled, and whoever humbles himself will be exalted" (Matthew 23:12, NIV).

Keepsake Box

Searching through a box for something I have since forgotten, I started reading notes, cards, and letters that I saved (some for many years) from people who have marched in my life's parade.

"If anything happens to me, these things should be kept," I said to the husband wielding the remote control. His surprising answer switched my mind into replay.

"Okay," he said, "but I suggest you enjoy them now. The significance of all of that stuff is gone when you are. No one else could put faces to those signatures or know what prompted the writing."

He was right. The value of the saved notes was what they kindled within me. Out of that box appeared faces I might otherwise never have visualized again. The kindness of them boosted my self-esteem, and the recollections made my eyes sting with tears. Some were neat, grammatically correct notes and others almost unreadable, but each one expressed gratitude for a small word or deed on my part. My friend, older and childless, was pleased to have had someone stand in for a daughter at a Mothers' Day party. A young woman recalled something at just the appropriate time that she had learned in my Sunday School class years before. A student, handicapped by a long illness, had utilized the encouragement given him in regard to his future. One friend thanked me for a moment of humor injected at an awkward moment. They were all such small things.

My mother, so careless about many things, had not neglected to instill in me the importance of writing acknowledgments. She was adamant. Over the years I did as I was taught, but I never thought of the notes as gifts or as an opportunity to uplift, inspire, or encourage. I returned the bulging keepsake box to its corner of the closet with a new understanding of Mother's insistence, with a new purpose in my correspondence, and with a determination to keep about my Father's work.

"A word fitly spoken is like apples of gold"
(Proverbs 25:11).
"For out of the overflow of the heart the mouth speaks"
(Matthew 12:34, NIV).

It's Here Somewhere

I gave my mother a suitcase once, but it didn't do any good. It was impossible for her to keep her things together in such a small place, and most of what she brought when she visited would not go in a suitcase anyway. The few clothes she brought fit fine in a clothesbasket, which is where they probably already were.

When Mother arrived for a visit, she came in the front door with both arms full and unloaded as she went from room to room. It took several such trips to empty the heavy-laden car. Thinking about it now, I can still feel the tension building in my stomach as I watched her transform my tidy house into a more "lived-in" one, as she called it. Amidst the clutter were always gifts for everyone, though not necessarily all in one piece or all in one place. "Don't worry," she would say, "the rest is in the car, I think. If not, I'll send it when I find it."

She also brought her latest hobby to show us, and her hobbies almost always involved paint in some form. The projects were never finished because she needed someone's opinion, which translated meant someone else to do it for her. I learned to do a lot of different crafts that way.

Once she arrived and unloaded, she considered her part of the work finished and was quite content to be treated as company. She did help with the cooking though, by preparing everyone's favorite dish to bring along. "That's

Tom's pie on the piano, and I made the casserole you like. Look in that box on the couch. I made Dean some rolls. They're here somewhere. I'm sure I brought them. Look in the car."

Mother had a reputation for losing things and for days after she left, I found them. When the time came to go through Mother's things, I found her marriage certificate dated more than fifty years earlier, my original birth announcement (almost as old), and a priceless letter from my Dad written from a beach in Okinawa during World War II. I didn't find these keepsakes tied up with a ribbon and put safely away, though. They were tucked here and there among empty envelopes, junk mail, greeting cards from friends, 10-year-old bank statements, newspaper clippings, belts from dresses she no longer had, and various other junk. No one knew her system, but it obviously worked. I'm organized but I have no idea where to find my children's birth announcements.

I was determined from an early age not to grow up to be like my mother. Now I wonder why. What could be so wrong about being happy-go-lucky, loved by everyone, and, like the Apostle Paul, content whatever your lot in life?

Changing Places

Mother was always busy. She worked hard all week and looked forward to the weekend when she could spend her small amount of free time in the garden or reading. Often she didn't get to do either, and that is when she got impatient with my grandmother who also looked forward to the weekend when Mother could take her to town. With careful planning Grandmother could usually make the grocery shopping and errand running last most of the day. At my age, nothing my grandmother did seemed very important to me, and just staying home, as mother seemed so anxious to do, was even less appealing.

All of that, however, was before I changed places with my mother. Before I knew what had happened, the house, the meals, the laundry, the budget, and the unexpected were lined up waiting their turn while I delivered children to lessons, watched ball games, and helped with homework. I wiped tears while holding back mine, and comforted hurts while my own went unattended. I said, "Yes," to being homeroom mother, heading up the fundraiser, and baking cookies, when I wanted to shout, "No!" I stayed up late administering solace to broken hearts and creating a costume for a last minute starring role. More than once, I recalled that young girl who thought staying home alone on Saturday was the pits.

Through it all, I acquired a greater respect for my mother and a genuine appreciation for her gift of giving, but unfortunately not a lot of patience. In the meantime, my mother had traded places with my grandmother. She no longer enjoyed time alone. She wanted mine.

I keep looking at myself and seeing my mother's reflection. It used to happen occasionally, but lately I remind myself more and more of her by the things I say and do. I even feel sometimes as though my children are looking at me through the same eyes I used to see her. That frightens me because I was often critical. Sometimes I feel as though I'm watching a performance that I have seen before, but this time I'm playing the role of my mother. My husband and my mother had a few issues on which they could never find common ground, so now when he calls me by my mother's name I know I'm pushing the limits.

When I was a young mother, I vowed to myself that I would not make the same mistakes my mother made. Now that I have changed places with her, I see things quite differently. Things she did, like talk to strangers in elevators, in lines, and on the street, embarrassed me profoundly. "Why does she do that?" I asked myself. I guess it wasn't such a bad thing after all, or I wouldn't now be doing it myself. Another annoying habit she had was bragging on her children. I know now that she did it because hers were exceptional, like mine.

I understand now that Mother wasn't as naive and unaware of what was going on around her as she appeared. Her theory was that what she didn't see she didn't have to do anything about, so she only saw what really mattered. I thought my mother was careless about her appearance, but now I suspect it was because there wasn't time or money left to spend on herself after she made sure the rest of us were shined and polished. The big hurt came when I realized that she actually had feelings. I made that discovery while trying to ignore the exchange of big sighs and raised eyebrows between my children when I said or did something dumb. More importantly, I wish I had realized sooner that parents don't lose their sense of identity along with their memories.

I often wish I had really listened to the stories Mother told us about her childhood and other bits and pieces from the past. Now I know that it is only when I'm asked, not when I volunteer information, that I have an attentive audience. How I wish my vision had cleared sooner.

Now, I'm the grandmother and with my new position came wisdom. Just ask me; I have all the answers, and I have many things planned for the weekends when my children have free time.

I have heard it said when an old person dies it is like a library burning. If so, that which remains is only what we, who are left, have preserved in our hearts and minds.

"Is not wisdom found among the aged? Does not long life bring understanding" (Job 12:12, NIV).

And the Winner Is...

In this conversation that I overheard, who do you think was the winner, Manipulation or Persuasion? You decide.

"Oh, Mom, you can't be serious," he said, knowing all the time that she was.

"Why not?" she asked.

"Because," he said emphatically, "nobody does that."

"You could be the first."

He hated it when she acted cute. "And the last," he said, "because I'd die of embarrassment."

"No you wouldn't," she said, patting him on the arm as if he was still nine years old instead of nineteen. That was one of her little mannerisms that put him on guard.

"Well, I would want to," he said. "I would pray to."

"Are you ashamed of her?" his mother asked, eyebrows rising in feigned shock.

"I didn't say that." Little did she know how proud he was of his sister.

"She looks and acts better than most of the girls you take out," his mother continued.

Familiar with that frequently made reference, he replied with obvious sarcasm, "Yeah, I know. She's Miss Perfect. Another Doris Night."

"Doris Day," she corrected, ignoring the implication.

"Well, whatever. I'm not taking her. Besides, she

wouldn't even want me to. Where do you come up with these ideas anyway?" He turned around hoping to walk away from the whole conversation.

"It was her idea," his mother said, following him.

He was struggling to keep his voice even. Whenever he lost his temper with his mother, he always suffered for it. It was a self-inflicted punishment. "Then why didn't she ask me? Why are you stirring around in it?"

"She was afraid to ask you," his mother replied.

"Oh, come on, she isn't afraid of anything."

"She was afraid you would say no."

"That's hard to believe. No one has ever told her 'no' in sixteen years."

"Why do you talk like that? Sometimes I think you're jealous of her," and then, in the voice reserved for just this subject, she added, "Remember, you had a dad for a while at least and she never has."

"And what does that have to do with this?"

"Well, he was better at saying no than I am."

"Gosh, Mom! I wish you'd make up your mind. One day I'm lucky he left and the next day I'm lucky I had him. I think it all depends on what you're trying to get me to do."

"Why that's terrible," she said accusingly, "you know I never ask anything of you that I can do myself. And it's obvious that I can't be her date." Then again, touching him, she said, "Why dear, I'll bet you'd even have a good time."

"Mom, I can't believe that you're serious about this. I couldn't."

And the Winner Is...

"I am and you could," she said.

"I can't and I won't." He was weary of this often-played game with his mother. A game he knew he couldn't win.

"You mean you want to think about it, don't you?"

"No, I don't want to think about it! No, I don't want to go! Why can't she get her own date like everyone else?"

"Because, young men today don't want to take out nice girls. You should know that." She smiled and he flinched.

"There must be some nerd around."

"Well, the last time she went out she had to drive her date home, if that tells you anything."

"You let her go out with a lush?" his anger surfacing.

"Well, he seemed nice, but you see what I mean. Anything could happen to her, but I wouldn't worry if she were with you."

She was doing it again and he felt helpless to stop it. "I wish you would stop battering me."

"And I wish you would think more about her and less about yourself. You know she thinks you can do no wrong. That makes you responsible in a way, don't you think?"

"Oh, now I am allowed to think?"

Accustomed to his wisecracks, she sighed significantly and continued, "Besides, she's already told all her friends that you're taking her."

"She shouldn't have done that because I am not!"

"Well, you'll have to tell her. I don't even want to be around when you do. I can't believe you care so little for her feelings."

That was it. She was moving in for the kill. "Mom,

will you lay off? I know exactly what you're doing. Where is this thing going to be anyway?" He wished he were not losing ground.

"Marion Civic Center."

"Way over there? Why not in the gym?"

"I don't know. I just know I'll be sick with worry. I won't be able to rest until she's home, unless she's with you."

He saw the end in sight. "You're trying to bridle me with guilt, aren't you, Mom?"

"No, I am not. That's the last thing I would do. My mother used to do that to me and I always said I would never do it to my children. I just think you should know that if you don't take her she'll miss one of the biggest events of the school year."

"No wonder he left."

"What?"

"I said it's time I left."

"Then you will!" came the victory cry.

"Well."

"I knew all the time you would do the right thing. Now don't you feel good?"

"Sure I do. As good as I can with a bit in my mouth." He turned toward the stairs, shoulders sagging and called, "Sis. . ."

Move Along...

On holidays I miss my parents. For one reason, the racks of beautiful greeting cards in every store, including the grocery, call out to me. While browsing through them I always hesitate at the sections with cards for mothers and fathers, until my consciousness thumps me and I remember that I no longer have either. There's a strange sorrow that passes over me briefly. It's a little like getting a shot. A quick, brief pain and life goes on.

The Gift of Love

Years ago when my brother was stationed in Japan he sent my mother a box of tiny, intricate, handmade ivory figurines. When they arrived she was recovering in the hospital and before I could retrieve them, she had given all but two of the unique exquisite treasures away to various staff members who had been "so nice to her." Unfortunately, I was not as happy about her sharing as she was, as is probably obvious by the fact that I'm still talking about it all these many years later. I could not make her understand that it would have been nice to have shared them with those of us in the family who knew him. No, she had her own order of importance. Another time we were shopping together when a clerk in a department store complimented her on a pin she was wearing, and Mother took the pin off and gave it to the admiring stranger—no matter that it had been a gift from me. How could I be cross with her, seeing how much joy that brought her? Talk about a cheerful giver!

I guess we all know that not everyone has a giving heart. I have known a Scrooge or two and remember a co-worker who would walk to work in a cold rain before she would ask another to give her a ride. That gave me an idea of how she felt about being asked for help. She would tell you that she didn't give and didn't expect anything from others. I felt sorry for her. She threw no bread on

The Gift of Love

the water and expected none to come to her. On the other side of the coin, growing up, we shared everything and not always by choice. Friends and neighbors stopped by our house without being invited or even calling first. If it was mealtime, all the better. To my mother, food was just another word for love, and even when it seemed we scarcely had enough for the family, she always insisted company stay and eat. My husband thinks to this day that Mother had Elijah helping in the kitchen. Not only did we share with others and help others and trust others, but they did the same with us.

I never heard of a homeless person when I was a child, but from time to time, someone would move in with us for a period of time and then move on. My grandmother fixed hot meals for men she called hobos or tramps in exchange for handiwork, and she often took food to old people she knew. There was a widowed lady in the neighborhood that everyone looked after, and fathers and big brothers carried in coal and carried out ashes for those who couldn't do it for themselves. If someone was ill, a neighbor or a friend attended to them or cared for their children until they were well. Thinking about it now, it was like a network that everyone belonged to. One person had a knack for one thing and someone else for another. If someone had more than they needed, they shared. No one kept track. No one was more important than another, no one talked about what they had done and over a period of time, almost everyone had a turn of helping and a turn of needing help.

That was *then*. This is *now*. You may be expecting me to say next, "But things are different now," and *things* are different now, but *love* is the same, and where there is love there is still the gift of giving.

There are more of us now, more conveniences, more opportunities, and more pitfalls, maybe, but nothing has altered our need for one another. Nothing has been discovered to replace the helping hand, the sympathetic ear, the comforting embrace, or the shelter of a friend's abode. We behave differently, we value different things, and we spend our time differently. We laugh a lot at styles and customs of the past, but our hearts are still attached to the same hub that they always have been–our families, our friends, our faith, our fellowman, and we still take care of that which we love.

In both the nation and the communities, we support organizations that minister to those who need help. We do so both by giving of our resources and by giving of our time, energy, and talents. When necessary, we respond to the needs of friends, neighbors, and strangers. Our church is a band of givers and doers always on the move looking after one another. While one member is preparing food for a hungry family, another shows up at the door with a hammer and saw wearing a nail apron and a big smile. Someone else brings his truck to move some donated furniture while a group of young people make a day out of painting or cleaning house for the homeless family to move into. Others are on call to deliver the sick for appointments or to make sure the lonely get out of the

The Gift of Love

house occasionally. Bereaved families are comforted and fed. Anonymous givers restore discontinued services. Compassionate souls visit the confined, and musicians play and sing to lift the spirits of the elderly or the ill. While these gifts of love are being spread around us all the time, no one is bragging or patting themselves on the back. While the spotlight naturally shines on some of the givers more than others, many are quietly doing their good work with only God as a witness. There are those whose gift is praying, while others write letters of hope and encouragement, or use the phone as a mission tool. The families of our ministers adjust their daily schedules often to accommodate the needs of others. A listening friend is a priceless gift. The list goes on.

I was fortunate to have learned the gift of love at home, and again from the Bible stories about the life of Jesus. I continue to have opportunities every day—as do we all—to be a *giver* and a *receiver* and to obey His command: "Love the Lord your God with all your heart and with all your soul and with all your mind.' This is the first and greatest commandment. And the second is like it: 'Love your neighbor as yourself.' All the Law and Prophets hang on these two commandments" (Matthew 22:37-40).

Part Two

My Heart Has A Green Thumb

Since childhood God has been as real to me as a bright, red poppy with its shiny black stamen, or a cluster of fragrant roses clinging to a tattered fence. He is still as near to me as a bird, a bug, or a bunch of violets. He reveals Himself to me in a tiny seed, a Pansy face, and the sound and smell of renewing rain. God teaches me object lessons with spiders and vines and oak trees. Every growing thing speaks to me of Him. This is a collection of things I have learned and written down to share with others whose love of growing things has acquainted them with God and those who also believe that He has given their heart a green thumb.

Spider In My Flower Pot

He was just a spider. Not a special variety or endangered or even brightly colored. He was in no way unique. I discovered him in the bottom of a flowerpot just as I was about to pour in the heavy, damp potting soil. I said to him, "Climb out of there little spider, before you get hurt." Then I turned the pot over and gave it a shake, but the spider held fast to the bottom of the pot. I gave it another shake and a bump with my hand. Still the spider didn't budge. "This is silly," I thought. "Why should I be concerned about an insignificant spider?" God answered my thought by reminding me of the times I had spent in dark depression, unwilling to turn loose in faith. I looked at that spider and saw myself there clinging desperately to false security. Then I tuned that spider's world upside down, as God had so often done to mine and shook him free of what he *thought* was best for him, into what I *knew* was best.

The Laughin' Place

Do you remember ol' Br'er Rabbit? If not, just check with Uncle Remus, and he will tell you all about that wise, old bunny and the Laughin' Place that God provided for him when life threatened. I think God provides us all with a laughing place, even if we go there to cry more often than to laugh. Do you know where your Laughin' Place is? Let me tell you about some I have known.

My dad was a real fisherman. The difference between a fisherman and a real fisherman is that the real one never gets tired fishing, never gives up, and doesn't have to catch anything to be happy. Real fishermen have faith, hope, and charity. They have faith that the fish are there, hope that they can catch them, and are very charitable about giving away the yet-to-be cleaned fish.

Dad was a skeptic when it came to religion. He tried hard to be a non-believer, but God got through to him in his Laughin' Place. Sitting out on the lake or gulf in his old fishing boat with the water softly slapping the sides of the boat, the simple things wore down his logic. It was the smell of the air and the water, the sound of the wind passing through the shoreline grasses, and the birds squawking overhead that he could not deny. Even the strange creatures he pulled from the depths belied his claim. If it hadn't been for his Laughin' Place, I think we would have lost him to Wormwood.[1]

My brother was a tough Army pilot. He liked to start arguments with me about my faith, but one day in a serious moment he assured me that no one could spend as much time as he had in the starry heavens without being a believer. He had found his Laughin' Place.

I was never a doubter. God has always been as near and as real to me as green plants and the rich earth they grow from. He speaks to me through bees and bugs and pansy faces. A garden is my Laughin' Place.

My mother always made her point with an object lesson. She didn't nag or preach, but simply found an example and left you thinking. I don't know if she learned it from God, or if He learned it from her, but God does the same to me in my Laughin' Place.

For years, I gathered Queen Anne's Lace from the roadsides in Tennessee, and attempted to grow it in my Florida garden. I brought home seedpods. I even brought Tennessee dirt to plant the seeds in, but they still didn't germinate. I brought home plants, but they died. It was all to no avail. Then one day when my heart was breaking over a situation in the life of one of my children, I was walking aimlessly in the garden, pleading with God for an answer when my eyes fell on blooming Queen Anne's Lace right in the middle of my flower border. I had weeded every inch of that flowerbed only a few days before. How could I have not seen a plant that size? While I stood there in disbelief watching the beautiful lacey white blooms

---

[1] *Screwtape Letters,* C.S. Lewis

The Laughin' Place

dance in slow motion to the tune of the breeze, I heard God say, "Wait." I knew right then that in His time the prayers for my child would be answered. Who knows how many times since then I have remembered that day and heard him say, "Wait."

After she passed, I brought Mother's amaryllis bulbs home (despite being left in a cardboard box by my back door all winter), yet in the spring they bloomed right where they were. They survived because God had already provided them with everything they needed. You can probably guess what. He told me that day. The same thing my mother had. "It's what's inside that counts."

Then there were the little oak seedlings. They were coming up thick under the tree where the big old oak and the squirrels had planted acorns. I pulled them up. Some came out easily with one hand while others made me pull at them with both. That object lesson said to me, "These little oaks are just like bad habits. They take root quickly and the longer they stay, the harder they are to get rid of."

From my chair in the family room, I can see activity at the pentis bush in my garden. Hummingbirds, butterflies, and bees gather there. "Why the pentis?" I wondered. "Because they are bright and cheerful," He said, "and always hospitable." "The same as I should be," I thought.

I'm not crazy about orange flowers for some reason. One summer an orange Gerbera daisy showed up in the front of the border right where I didn't like it. It was a strong, healthy plant and produced many blooms, but that orange bloom in the middle of pink ones really bothered me. I finally decided to move it, thinking that if it didn't survive it would not be a great loss. "Is that anything like asking some people to sit in the back of the bus?" God asked. I didn't move the Gerbera. I left it for a reminder.

The object lessons are a daily occurrence. Others may not see them as divine inspirations like I do, but I know from the Bible that God spoke to His children in many ways, and just maybe it was sometimes with an object lesson taught in their Laughin' Place.

If you haven't already, find yourself a Laughin' Place and spend some real quality time listening to your Heavenly Father.

"Happy are those who listen to me, watching at my door every day" (Proverbs 8:34).

Giant Oaks and Little Sins

In the cool shade of an old oak in my backyard live a variety of ferns and wildflowers. They thrive there in the rich moist soil with the branches overhead measuring their sunshine. They are undisturbed except when the big oak, at the season's signal, drops acorns in their bed.

One morning while I was weeding out the resulting seedlings I was distracted by unfamiliar sounds. The commotion was coming from heavy equipment and a crew of workmen preparing to remove four giant oaks from in front of my house. The stately trees were beautiful. Their heavily foliaged limbs reached across the curving street to join hands with their own kind on the other side, creating an inviting tunnel of shade. But as appealing as they were, on the inside where their strength should have been, they were in fact hollow and rotten. This discovery had recently been made at great expense when a similar tree dropped a giant limb on a passing car. I watched a long time while men and machines wrestled with the huge trees and wondered why I so hated to see them go despite their danger.

It was nearly a week before the work was completed, and some days it looked as if the skilled workmen would lose the battle. When the trees were finally uprooted, like extracted giant teeth, it seemed their roots had gone as deeply into the ground as their branches had reached skyward. One stubborn tree, completely hollow, refused to give up its hold. Instead, it broke off at the ground and left its roots permanently behind. Only after the trees were hauled away, the holes filled, and the grass replanted, did the quiet return. Even then, the scars remained.

The next time I knelt in the shade of the big oak to weed out the newly sprouted trees, my thoughts returned to those giant oaks that had begun as small as these. How well disguised, I thought, was the ultimate potential of the randomly planted acorns. In a moment of unexpected awe I paused to look up through the filtering leaves and sent a thought of thanks.

I returned then to my weeding, but my mind lingered. I guess I'm not a lot different from the oaks. I pulled up the smallest of the trees with one hand and tugged with both on the more established ones. Life is always planting seeds in my life, too. Some are flowers and some are weeds. What is allowed to root is up to me.

Like little oaks, sin crops up unbidden. It is subtle and seemingly insignificant in the beginning, but left alone, quickly puts down deep roots. It is often quite appealing and flaunts beguiling comforts that make me reluctant to relinquish it. It isn't easily contained, and can grow immense and spread its resulting branches over others.

I remembered the workmen's long hard struggle to remove the diseased trees left so long unrestrained. I thought about the roots that would not budge and the scars left from those that did. I recalled the tragic consequences suffered by the innocent bystanders.

No longer can I sit in the shade of the old oak tree and idly pull up the tiny seedlings without thinking about the garden of my own life.

Bloom Where You Are

If you are a gardener, you already know the importance of talking to your flowers. Mostly, I praise them. "You smell so fragrant today," I sometimes tell them, or "What a large bloom you've made!" They like it when I comment on how nice their foliage looks, or thank them for providing so many blooms just when I need them.

On and on it goes. They even lift up their pretty flower faces and smile back at me. Occasionally I have to get stern with one or another of them, but they usually perk right up afterwards. That's not all. The flowers talk back to me. They always have since I was a little girl, and you might be surprised how much I have learned from them.

Recently I overheard a conversation while walking alone along a path in the woods. It was quiet except for a few leaves skipping along with me in time with the breeze and a bird or two dropping a musical note now and then. At first, when I heard the voices, I thought I was no longer alone, but I looked in every direction and saw no one. What I was hearing were the wildflowers and weeds discussing their uppity relatives grown in nurseries and hot houses.

"So where do those hybrids think they got their start in the first place?" asked Queen Anne in a haughty voice, her beautiful lace gently blowing in the breeze. "Pulled themselves up by their own root stock, did they?"

"Don't they know that left to themselves they would

soon be common again?" Daisy called down from her tall stem.

"You're just jealous," said Violet, a bold statement from one so shy. "I would love to live in a beautiful glass house and be watered ever so gently with a fine mist on my leaves rather than by raindrops that knock me down."

"Me, too," joined in Wild Rose, "and go to church on the lapel of a lovely lady, or to the prom and dance on the arm of a young girl in love."

"Oh, you two are such dreamers!" replied Queen Anne. "Do you know how short-lived that glory would be? I'd rather have a bee on my shoulder."

"She's right," said Sweet Clover. "And just think, they may never have even seen a sunrise, or felt a cool breeze. I don't suppose they even know what the moon looks like."

"But don't forget the storm beatings we have to take and the long periods without a drop of water," added Dandelion.

"Yeah, and they never get walked on either," replied Clover, "or run over with that terrible cutting machine."

"They do get pruned though. I've heard that sometimes they have all but one of their buds removed just to see how large a flower they can make," Moss Rose said with a shudder.

After more grumbling among them, I heard Jack-in-the-Pulpit say, "Now don't be unkind, the Master Gardner made nothing common. We are what we are and where we are to serve His purpose."

"Tell us then, why are we not valued more, but

considered good only for covering the fields and ditches where we're walked upon and called weeds? Why do others look down on us, and why are we never gathered into bouquets to be placed in palaces?" Queen Anne asked.

"Weeds and wildflowers have their own special place and purpose. We decorate the countryside and provide food and shelter for His creatures. Our gift of beauty is available to people of every circumstance," he replied. "Why can't you be happy and content where you're planted? You're starting to sound like humans."

And isn't that the truth? Some of us do grumble a lot about where we are planted and how we compare with others. If you have ever felt like a flower in a weed patch, or a weed in a flower garden as I have, remember that whatever your variety and wherever you are growing, God is the Master Gardener and He wants you to bloom where you are planted.

"Each one should use whatever gift he has received to serve others, faithfully administering God's grace in its various forms" (1 Peter 4:10, NIV).

The Importance of Mud Pies

It has been a long time since I made a real mud pie. I guess growing up in a time and a home where domestic skills were highly valued, it was natural for me to enjoy playing house and creating lavishly decorated pies and cakes from whatever dirt, leaves, and flowers I could stir up. I remember mixing the Indiana black soil and water into wonderful chocolate confections and decorating them with flowers to serve at the weddings of my Hollyhock dolls.

By the time I was transplanted in Florida, I had advanced beyond mud to real ingredients, and that was a good thing because Florida doesn't have dirt, only sand. As you know, sand and water don't make mud. I have watched water puddle up and float on top of dry sand. I have seen dry spots remain in the yard following a downpour, and water run off the surface of a flowerbed like off a duck's slick back. I sat in on an agriculture class once while the instructor explained to the students that it was necessary when planting a citrus tree to "mud-it-in." To my surprise, he was using my old mud pie recipe. He instructed them to first fill the hole with water and then gradually add sand while mixing it with their hands until it was thoroughly saturated.

Those mud pies came to my mind again the day my friend returned an African violet that she had been plant sitting for me while I was away. The violet was limp and very sad-looking. My friend began immediately to explain how she had watered it but that the water just ran out the drainage hole in the bottom as fast as she poured it in the top. I assured her that it would survive and put it to soak in the kitchen sink. What I knew (that she didn't know I knew) is that she allowed it to dry out completely before resuming the watering, and that totally dry dirt resists water. I knew that from having done the same thing, and not with just my plants.

For periods of time, I sometimes allow my spiritual life to suffer from drought. When that happens, I can sit in a church pew and receive not one inspirational thought from a sermon that is inspiring those around me. After a church service, I have heard others giving kudos to the choir for an outstanding musical performance while I didn't even know what the choir had sung. I have tried with no success to get interested in an inspirational book that my friends were recommending. Sometimes my Bible reading even becomes mechanical and nothing jumps out at me with significance. It seems like my soul has become nonabsorbent. The worst part of being spiritually dry is while in that frame of mind, prayer is empty and unsatisfying. No wonder the violet looked sad. In that condition, I'm sad too.

How do I get that way? The same as the violet did, from neglect. Without the constant renewal of my soul that comes from prayer, Bible reading, the companionship of Christian friends, and serving others, I dry up spiritually.

The Importance of Mud Pies

The less I water my soul with worship, the less absorbent I become.

In order to recondition the violet, I placed the container in water with nutrients and let it absorb all it could hold, and I keep it vibrant and blooming by never allowing it to get completely dry.

How about me? How do I prevent my own spiritual wilting? I have learned that the more I pray, the better I pray. The more I read the Bible, the more I think, and the more I worship in any form, the happier I am. The more time I spend in the company of other Christians the more I grow. The more time I spend with the Lord, the more beautiful the bloom.

I believe that nothing good is ever wasted, even child's play. Many things I learned as a child are still important today, mud pies included.

"Draw nigh to God, and He will draw nigh to you" (James 4:8).

Resurrection

It was Good Friday. I felt a little guilty about working in the yard instead of doing something religious, but because I'm good at rationalizing things to my own advantage, I concluded that being outside with nature was a form of worship.

It was an exceptionally beautiful morning. The sky was soft blue with puffs of white about. The breeze was cool enough to make me enjoy the warm sun on my back, and a Great Crested Flycatcher was singing his favorite song with vigor in the budding oak behind me. God's presence was as real to me as the damp dirt I was digging in. It was a *good* Friday.

My project for the morning was to transplant some coreopsis seedlings, from the crowded bed where last summer's fireworks of bloom had re-seeded them, into a spot that needed a touch of yellow. Even though I tried not to disturb the roots, very soon they were lying limp in their new bed. Later that day the Lord showered them with a Good Friday downpour, but on the following overcast day they looked like crumpled paper. Disappointed, I gave them up and regretted the time I had wasted.

Early Sunday morning I made my routine trip around the house opening blinds and curtains. When I glanced through the bedroom window, the first thing I saw was the transplants. The same ones I had given up on yesterday

Resurrection

were standing up briskly in the sunshine. One even had a little color peeking out.

I don't know why I was so surprised. It *was* Easter morning!

Mine To Keep

Nine-fifteen and the sun is just showing itself over the mountain. Down the hill, through shades of green, the Little River is still wearing its morning cloak of fine-spun mist. Eagerly on its way, wherever it is going, the rushing water is playing a rhapsody over and around the river rocks.

While the birds are giving a concert in the surrounding trees, an amorous cricket is singing a solo from his secret place. From a blue sky sunlight is shining through a filtering canopy of whispering leaves, and the shadows are dancing on the grass in ever-changing choreography. Tall and erect above the others, one tree stands with giant limbs extended as if it were the proud conductor of this melodious silence.

The wildflowers around the doorstep are all refreshed from their morning shower and the day's parade of little creatures has begun. The air is sweet and thick with the flavor of woods and water and I want to inhale enough to last forever. But, I cannot. I am but a guest here. Nothing is mine to take away with me, except the memory. That is mine to keep.

". . .And God saw everything that He had made, and behold, it was very good" (Genesis 1:31).

Tender Shoots

The sidewalk was steamy hot outside the drugstore, and I was anxious to get back to my car. However, before I could, I felt compelled to pick up a long tendril of new growth trailing over the edge of a brick planter and resting on the hot cement sidewalk. Otherwise, it would surely perish from the heat or from being trampled by passing feet. As soon as I let loose of the repositioned tendril, it unwound itself and returned to the same precarious path. While I was deciding what to do next to rescue the determined sprout, a young man passed by gently tugging the hand of a crying child also obviously reluctant to go where he was being led. I felt a smile escape and thought, "We have similar problems." I knew from experience that directing new growth required very careful handling, be it vine or child.

The moment brought to mind the task that I had taken on years before-training vines to cover the lattice over our patio. I planted the fast-growing plants next to each of the posts, and impatiently watched as they put down roots and sent out new shoots. As soon as the tendrils became long enough, I began rearranging them to grow in the direction I thought was best. I wound them in and out of the lattice slats, sometimes forcing them against their natural inclination or securing them until they complied. Other times I twisted them together with another tendril that was already headed in the right direction. Even when I was very gentle, the tender shoots sometimes snapped and from time to time, I had to prune them into compliance. The vines flourished, despite a freeze now and then, a hurricane or two, and various other attacks by nature. In return for my persistence, they eventually rewarded me with a shaded patio and with sweet fragrant blooms. All of that was back during the same busy years that I was attempting to shape the lives of a teenager, an adolescent and a baby.

Time passed. The vine grew and no longer needed my continuous supervision, which was good, because it had grown beyond my reach anyway. It twists and turns on its own established branches now. It blooms, sheds its blooms, and produces new growth all on schedule–regardless of me. So it is with my grown children. During the years it took that vine to grow beyond my reach, my children did the same. Now I am sheltered under their protection and showered with pride and satisfaction.

While there is no comparison between the importance of training plants and training children, there are some similar principles. When the vine on the hot sidewalk rewound into its position of choice, and the little boy pulled in the opposite direction from his father, it reminded me of the many times I had to deal with resistance from my own children. I thought of all my strategies to discourage unwanted behavior. From potty training on, there were always new ways they tried to evade me or to avoid the rules. We tried to encourage friends from within acceptable

Tender Shoots

borders that would help lead them in the right direction, but occasionally a stray took root. In addition to their physical care, their mental and spiritual development also required a lot of twisting and turning during those formative years. The hardest part of all was the necessary pruning required from time to time.

Thinking about it now, I realize that the analogy that God put in my mind that day also applies to my own life. Scripture tells me that the Master Gardener had a plan for my life before I had a life. Remembering, I know that I was a weed growing wild in His garden until He lovingly cultivated me. The things in my life that were such disappointments, the things I thought were unfair hardships, the plans I had that never came to be, and the painful pruning that I encountered, were all for my own good and were necessary before I could put out new growth and fill my place in His Garden of Life.

I am but one of God's tender sprouts. Look around, they are everywhere. I pray that together we may create a beautiful garden to attract others to Him.

> *"Trust in the Lord with all your heart and lean not unto your own understanding. In all thy ways acknowledge Him and he will direct your paths" (Proverbs 3:5-6).*

My Friendship Garden

If you want to see a Rosarian squirm, just ask which is their favorite rose. They may come up with a name but more than likely not a one-word answer. It might go like this, "The rose that I think is the most beautiful color doesn't have much fragrance. The most fragrant of the roses tends to have crooked stems. I like another for its long vase life if you don't mind a lot of thorns. Another is the best show rose but is very difficult to grow." On and on that might continue, "this one is disease resistant, that one makes a lot of blooms, and this variety is my choice for landscaping…"

Ask a bird watcher which is the most outstanding species and get the same conditional response, or a chef his favorite recipe, a musician his favorite song, or a librarian her favorite book. In most cases there are also as many reasons to dislike something in particular. I understand this because decisions are very difficult for me, and to make it even more frustrating, I change my mind frequently. If I were asked to choose a favorite friend, no doubt I would find myself in a similar dilemma.

In my flower garden I have cultivated a lot of different varieties over the years. In many ways the flowers remind me of the friendships I have also developed during the same years. Some flourish, some suffer from neglect, some survive but do not thrive. There are those I keep trying

My Friendship Garden

to make bloom despite their aggravating traits, and a few I have let wither and die. I even find myself comparing flowers and personalities.

The roses are among my favorites because they give so much beauty and fragrance to the garden and provide me with bouquets when I need them, just like those friends who lift my spirits and are always available if I need them.

The daylilies come and go quickly, but at just the right time. They bloom in the morning and are gone by dark, but they have made my day brighter, like a friend dropping in unexpectedly. The azaleas remind me of those faithful, long-time friends I see infrequently but still hold close in heart even when they are not blooming at my doorstep. I have quiet friends I almost forget. Like shy violets, they stay in the background until I seek them out. Just today there is a bold red amaryllis in the flower border partially blocked from view but calling my attention to the weeding I have been neglecting. I most definitely need an assertive friend on my team. The brightly colored pentis are the friendliest shrubs in the garden. They attract a constant flight of butterflies and bees coming and going and remind me of my very busy friends that always have time for others. I have some thorny flowers in my garden also, and some temperamental ones. I have to handle them carefully, just like difficult people, but they all have something that makes them worth keeping.

Then, there are the weeds. I'm not sure who designated which was a flower and which was a weed, but I think a few were misnamed, because nothing adds to a bouquet like Queen Anne's Lace. Besides, the weeds keep me on my knees, and are so hardy I have to admire their determination. The flowers and the weeds growing side by side in the garden remind me of a quote by Edward Wallis Hoch, "There is so much good in the worst of us, and so much bad in the best of us, that it hardly behooves any of us to talk about the rest of us."

Neither my flowers nor my friendships are self-sustaining. Flowers need sunshine, water, and nutrients to grow and bloom. Friendships require nurturing calls, occasional visits, shared laughter, and tears. Friendship requires secure confidences, encouragement, tolerance, and forgiveness. Friends, like flowers, even need to be pruned on occasion.

I talk a lot with the Master Gardener while I am in the garden. He assures me that I need not choose favorites, because each variety of flower and friend He created for me to love and enjoy excels in its own way. Each is its own reward for the time spent cultivating.

"For there is no respect of persons with God" (Romans 2:11).

Part Three

What Happens When I Stop, Look, and Listen

Since I was a little child God has been telling me stories and teaching me with object lessons. I often write down these conversations with God… lest I forget.

Lest I Forget

Do you ever wonder if God spends as much time with all his children as He does with you? I do. He just won't leave me alone. He talks to me, He nudges me, He reminds me, He scolds me, He paints pictures in my mind's eye, and He stirs my heart.

At night when I am tucked in and comfortable in my bed, He makes me think of all the people who have no crisp sheets in the summer or warm blankets in the winter to cozy up in, and those who have no bed at all. Sometimes when I eat too much and feel uncomfortable, my calorie counting is interrupted with a vision of hungry children.

While I watch the news at the end of the day from my favorite chair in our safe, comfortable, air-conditioned home, I see men fighting in the streets, children huddled in cold barren hovels, and women overworked and hopeless. He makes me thankfully aware of the peaceful life I live. When I try to organize all that I have accumulated and complain about having no room left to put it all, He asks me when will I have enough. I'm embarrassed and ashamed.

Reading books and writing letters are favorite pastimes for me, and I can scarcely imagine what it must be like not knowing how to read, having nothing available to read, or no leisure time to read, He keeps urging me to share my love of words with others. When I am sick and stuck in bed with pills to take instead of busy doing things I had planned, when I am awake all night waiting for a child's fever to break, or when my failing parents need me yet again, He brings to mind all those who have no help or hope and makes me compassionate.

On occasion I have grumbled about working, but then quickly retreated when reminded of all the people who don't have jobs. While I make budgets and stretch my money, God points out to me how much I have compared to nothing at all, and He provides me with an opportunity to share. When I say, "no," to a responsibility at church, He sends a missionary to show me real commitment.

Society likes to smooth my conscience and tell me I'm okay. Scholars attempt to explain away my guilt. Over-exposure to little white lies, dishonest deals, callous conversations, and sensual sins dull my senses. Because He has blessed me so, I start to feel like I must be okay, but only until I open my Bible and He reads to me from the pages of history and points out the consequences of sin and complacency.

Sometimes I look at other people and think I know what is wrong with them. When I'm impatient with another but satisfied with myself, He is the referee and I don't always win the round. He opens my eyes and lets me see myself as I really am, and keeps me humble. All of this is nothing new to me, and I would never change a thing. I first sensed His presence when I was a little girl, and He has had me covered ever since. As long as I can remember, God has been lovingly tutoring me. He never leaves me alone.

"From heaven, the Lord looks down and sees all mankind; from his dwelling place he watches all who live on earth—He who forms the hearts of all, who considers everything they do" (Psalm 33:13-15, NIV).

Squeeze of a Lifetime

I have always had an uncanny desire to change places briefly with another person in order to compare their thoughts and their feelings with mine. Judging from the reactions of others to some of my ideas, I'm beginning to doubt I'm a standard model. I especially wonder if the need I have to give meaning to everything I experience is a common trait. Take the toothpaste for example.

You know about toothpaste squeezers and toothpaste rollers, of course, and how much that reveals about a person. One look at my toothpaste tube and it is obvious that I'm a squeezer. Actually, I don't think like a squeezer though, because in my mind I always see myself rolling the next tube. Either way, that commonplace object has become symbolic to me of time. Every day I have less.

Each time I start fresh with a brand new tube of toothpaste, all neat and fat and full, I do the same thing. I use a lot. Sometimes I even lather twice; imagine that waste! As the tube gets thinner and thinner, I begin to use less and less in order to make it last longer. Even when it appears to be all gone, I can still manage by twisting and squeezing to get enough to brush one more time. While I'm turning that tube inside out to get the last possible vapor, I'm thinking regretfully about the gobs I started out using and make that same promise to do better with the next tube. I have even stopped buying the large economy

Squeeze of A Lifetime

size, knowing that the more I have the more I will use.

I do the same thing with time. I waste it.

Time. What is it anyway? You can't see it, touch it, or feel it. You can't hold it back or speed it up. No rocket scientist in the world can alter it, and it can't be contained or recycled. Try as I may, there is no way to know how much I still have.

Time is a gift from God with no strings attached. It is mine to use as I choose, to invest or to squander. It can buy me satisfaction or regret, accomplishment or destruction, friends or enemies. I may spend it any way I want. More than once while sorting the remaining belongings of an older person I have discovered gifts, cherished, but unused, carefully put away for later. How many treasured items am I saving to use on special occasions that may never come? How many good intentions have I put aside until I have more time? What about the secure nest egg tucked away for a rainy day while someone I love is suffering through a drought now? How much of what I exchange my time for is worth the time spent? Should I be giving a tithe of my time back to the Giver?

That tube reminds me each morning that time also runs out. I have squeezed life to the point where I can see the tube caving in. Worse yet, with the new-fangled containers you can't tell how much is gone and suddenly you are left with none. What I once used with abandon, I have started measuring out more carefully. I have also given some thought to the battered and abused container that holds me together. Careful rolling might extend its use. In my mind's eye, I can see myself doing things a lot differently if I could start over, but with life you only get one tube. Besides, it is amazing how much one can get out of an empty tube when you have spent a lifetime practicing. Now tell me, is that what you think about while you brush your teeth? I often wonder.

> *"There is a time for everything and a season for every activity under heaven..." (Ecclesiastes 3:1-14, NIV).*

The Lion In the Log

From my box of clippings and from a writer I'm unable to acknowledge, I found a short and profound story. It told about an artist who was whittling an old log. Over the summer he patiently removed slices, slivers, and chunks from the piece of rough wood while a neighbor child patiently watched his progress. When the young child returned from a few weeks of vacation, he found in place of the nondescript piece of wood a beautiful, smoothly polished lion. The boy gasped in amazement and asked, "How did you know he was in there?"

A couple familiar clichés came to my mind after reading about the lion in the log. I have often heard it said that "beauty is only skin deep," and more than once I have been drawn to a physically attractive person only to have that confirmed. Contrary to the cliché I have also learned that real beauty comes from deep inside, and with my eyes focused on the surface I have overlooked many treasures.

My first day of high school was also my first day in Florida and a day I will always remember. I had never felt as alone or as afraid as I did that morning while standing in the doorway of the huge old school. It wasn't because I was alone. There were hundreds of other students surrounding me, all laughing and chatting and having fun and all completely unaware of me. All, that is, except one person. I hadn't even noticed her before she approached me with a smile and swished me away to my first class. Despite her pretty face, she was chunky for a teenager, and her homemade dress wasn't stylish and it didn't fit well. It was obvious she hadn't spent nearly as much time getting ready for the first day of school as I had, and she definitely didn't reflect the covers of the then popular *Seventeen* magazines. In today's jargon, fat and frumpy would probably have been used to describe her.

For the remainder of that day and for a few weeks following, she was at my elbow each time I needed direction or felt confused. She introduced me to my teachers and to my first few friends. At lunchtime she was my guide through the cafeteria maze where even the food looked foreign, and at the end of the day she made sure I got on the right bus. As I learned my way around the school and made more friends, mostly forgotten by now, our paths began to cross less often because I needed her less. I'm afraid I never considered the possibility of her needing me. It was when she died much too young that I realized what I had so casually discarded. I will never know how many others she befriended in her short lifetime, but I do know that hidden within her was a beautifully polished treasure.

When I hear, "still water runs deep," I'm reminded of a seemingly shy young man in a class I was teaching who seldom spoke up, but who stirred me with his insight when he did. I always wanted to hear more of what he was thinking, and I still wonder what else was hidden in him undiscovered. Another polished treasure maybe?

The Lion In the Log

I know well that shops display the most attractive items in their store windows to get attention, and that dress shops hang the smallest dress sizes on the front of the racks because they are the most appealing. I also know that piled in the back of the store are the real bargains. Ever wonder how many beautiful people are hidden under the counters or on the back shelves because of their packaging? Each of us has within us something which makes us unique and special that is not always obvious in our outward appearance. God knows what is in there, but we must search for it in ourselves and in others.

"Each one should test his own actions. Then he can take pride in himself, without comparing himself to somebody else" (Galatians 6:4).

Measuring Up

If the merchant's scale is not balanced, someone will be cheated. If the contractor's corners are not square, the building will lean. If the tailor's measuring tape is stretched, the garment will not fit.

I'm five feet and two inches tall. How do I know? I have a yardstick. I know how much I weigh and I'm not telling, but the scales will. With highly accurate instruments, doctors can measure things they can't see. Since the beginning of time the world and all that is in it has operated by the laws of nature: the seas, the seasons, the sun, and the moon. The Bible is an instruction manual for living with no detail left to chance. God even devoted five chapters in the book of Exodus to provide exact details for building his Holy Tabernacle. *"He made the earth by his power; He founded the world by his wisdom and stretched out the heavens by his understanding" (Jeremiah 10:12, NIV).*

Having said all that about the importance of measurements, I find it amazing that God has given us such a simple guideline for forgiveness.

> *"Do not judge and you will not be judged. Do not condemn, and you will not be condemned. Forgive, and you will be forgiven. Give, and it will be given to you...For with the measure you use, it will be measured to you" (Luke 6:37-38, NIV).*

Measuring Up

He made it plain. As often as I pray the Lord's Prayer, am I not asking that God deal with me in the same way I choose to deal with others? Am I not deciding my own fate by asking Him to judge me by my own example? *"For if you forgive men when they sin against you, your heavenly Father will also forgive you. But if you do not forgive men their sins, your Father will not forgive your sins" (Matthew 6:14-15, NIV).*

It is scary when I think about it. Maybe it would be safer if I were praying that God be more understanding and forgiving with me than I am with others.

Forgiveness isn't always easy. When I'm called upon to forgive, it is sometimes the smallest things that are hardest for me to let go. Maybe that is because I don't really want to forgive, or because my pride is involved. I have observed that the undeserved hurts are the most difficult to give up. Neither does forgiveness come easily for me in those areas where I'm vulnerable and sensitive or have been hurt before. Then there are the deep, life-changing injuries that require God's helping grace to forgive. However, God didn't categorize. He simply stated, *"...But if you do not forgive men their sins, your Father will not forgive your sins" (Matthew 6:14-15, NIV).*

What makes me judgmental? Could it be that by putting another down I build myself up? Do I get some sense of satisfaction from finding fault, or do I just lack compassion? Does my impatience with others come from feeling superior, or is it just Satan's way of pushing me ahead of my own better judgment? What I really want is for Jesus to say in my behalf what He said from the cross. *"Father, forgive them for they do not know what they are doing" (Luke 23:34, NIV).*

Thinking about judgment and forgiveness brings to my mind a vision of standing in front of God on Judgment Day sometime in the future after this life is over. Actually, every day is a judgment day because forgiveness fixes things and the sooner the better. Forgiveness is healing, physically, mentally, and spiritually. It is like removing a splinter from a throbbing finger, putting down a heavy load, or taking a tonic. It gives peace of mind and opens up the lines of communication with God and others. Forgiveness makes it easier to understand and help one another.

I remember a simple story I was told a long time ago. A small boy went to his father and told him about something hurtful that he had done to his friend and which he now regretted. His father told him to get a nail and hammer it into a fence post and then go to his friend, tell him that he was sorry and do whatever was possible to make amends. Afterwards, he could remove the nail. The little boy did as he was told and then returned to his father and said, "I have done what you told me to do and have removed the nail, but the hole is still there." Then his father explained to him that every decision has a consequence, and he should always consider the consequence before making the decision because even when we have been forgiven the consequence remains.

My Prayer: Remind me Lord to be more forgiving, more tolerant, more patient, less judgmental, and to lay down the grudges which are weighing me down. Enable me to see others though your eyes and try harder to experience their feeling, so that my life and the lives of others will be better day by day. Help me to sow and cultivate that which I hope to reap. Amen.

Maze of Faith

Last night I had a vision. It appeared in the form of a maze similar to a wooden labyrinth, and looking down from above I could see the beginning, the end, and all the roads in between. The maze was full of children traveling from birth to adulthood. Some paths were smooth with gentle slopes and bright skies and the children on those roads appeared happy and carefree. Other roads were dark and foreboding. Many children were traveling those roads and coaxing others to join them. Evil guides lurked ready to point the young travelers toward wrong turns and dead ends. Other paths were baited for young appetites with enticing billboards that promised shortcuts to adult privilege.

The atmosphere in the maze changed frequently. The children appeared to be happy at times and then confused and afraid. Some of the frightened children called out while others seemed determined to go their own way despite the help they were offered. Many sat alone not attempting to advance at all. Then in the vision I saw myself there struggling with my children. To my dismay, they weren't on the smooth and pleasant road. I pointed them in the right direction, but they turned away. Though I could easily see dangers from my vantage point, they wouldn't listen to my warnings. I showed them the many good things along the way, but they weren't interested. I worried about all I saw and heard and imagined, and I suffered at their every mistake. I tried to protect them from every hurt, every disappointment, and every consequence. I pleaded with God for help while I franticly attempted to solve their problems.

God reached down, lifted me out of the maze, and set me on the sidelines. He had heard my prayers on their behalf. He was aware of my efforts to instruct them in His ways. He understood what I was experiencing. He knew how it felt to see His children suffer because they were disobedient, because they ignored the rules, and because they made poor choices. He had felt the hurt that came from disrespect and ungratefulness, and He reminded me that the more one loved the more one suffered. He knew all about suffering.

"Where is your faith?" He asked. "Why do you ask of me and not expect an answer?"

"I do have faith, Lord, but there's so much potential for harm and disappointment I cannot leave them here alone."

"You may have a beautiful voice, but until you sing there is no song. You may think great thoughts, but until you express them they accomplish nothing. You may have all the right ingredients, but until you combine them there is no cake. The action required of faith is that you trust Me. Just because you didn't see me embracing your children in the maze, didn't mean I wasn't."

I'm still watching closely as my children travel the Maze. I'm still instructing them and disciplining them as the Lord leads me. Even though I don't always understand the things that God allows or understand the way my children sometimes think, I have faith that they are in the hands of the Infallible Guide whose love for them far exceeds my own and I believe they will arrive safely.

"Now faith is being sure of what we hope for and certain of what we do not see" (Hebrews 11:1, NIV).

Everyday A New Beginning

I have no plans to go back to school any time soon and I don't need new pencils, pens, or notebooks, but every year at this time I get exhilarated when I see stores everywhere filling up with school supplies. What is it that makes even kids who don't like to go to school get anxious to shop for crayons, scissors, and notebooks? What makes me want to linger in those aisles and watch while parent and child, list in hand, excitedly pick and choose their favorites? I think it has to do with new beginnings.

I don't know which I anticipated most in the past, meeting my own new teacher on the first day of the school year or checking out the one who would be my child's teacher. Either way I knew it meant new adventures. The excitement may not have lasted long, but it was always there in the beginning. I even find it refreshing to turn over the calendar each month, a clean page with no scribbles and the promise of thirty more blank days to get it right. Isn't that what I am wishing when I say, "If I had it to do over?" Now that I think about it, my life is a series of new beginnings.

In January I customarily put aside mistakes of the past and resolve to do better with the New Year. Just when I need it, spring brings new weather accompanied by budding trees, baby birds, the rebirth of flowers and gardens, and an attitude adjustment. Most importantly spring brings

Easter, which represents the greatest new beginning of all. Soon afterward it is time for vacation, bringing with it a change of schedules, activities, and sometimes scenery. Before I know it, school supplies are back on the shelves!

I also know that not all changes or new beginnings are as welcome as the revolving seasons or as simple as a clean piece of paper. Some are frightening. Some are painful and disruptive. Sometimes new beginnings demand hard-to-make decisions made worse by fear of the unknown. That is when I have to remind myself that God knows things I don't know and that He uses all things for good. I recall times in the past when even the most difficult new beginnings resulted in blessings I never imagined. Then I flip through the pages of my Bible to see promise after promise I have underlined there.

The same God that got Noah, Abraham, and Moses where they needed to be is my Guide, too. God richly blessed Job for his faith, and I have faith. Even when Jonah was over his head and down in the mouth, God made sure everything came out alright for Jonah. I have been there. David messed up too, and God gave him a clean slate and a fresh start. The greatest missionary of all time started his new career with a dramatic new beginning. Why would God do less for me? Therefore, I claim this promise from Isaiah 26:3, *"Thou will keep him in perfect peace, whose mind is stayed on Thee..."*

I may not be going back to school any time soon, but I'm looking forward to the next chapter in my life's book.

Everyday A New Beginning

Affluence

I confess. I'm a window peeper. I never look in under shades, of course, but as I drive along at night I like to glance in through lighted windows.

Sometimes I notice a picture on the wall or see a family seated around a table, a flickering TV, or a mother busy behind a kitchen window. Sometimes those window scenes are so warm and inviting it makes me want to stop and visit.

One evening I was driving home from a visit with my grandchildren through one of those typically American middle class, middle income, young-family neighborhoods glancing at homes as I passed when a word suddenly popped into my mind. Affluence. Even in this neighborhood of young, working parents the evidence was apparent. Most homes I observed had at least two cars parked in the driveway. Their cars were there because their double-car garages were already full. Open garage doors revealed boats, boxes, benches, and bikes–racing bikes, motor-cross bikes, motorcycles, tricycles, and little pink bikes with flowers on the handlebars. I saw lawn mowers, power tools, exercise equipment, fishing gear, and water skis. Shelves lining the walls were piled high, and stacked boxes on the floor left only a tunnel to the door. I suspected that the houses were as full of things as the garages.

Then I came home and weaved my way through my

Affluence

own garage into the laundry room that was full of things I had no place for in my crowded closets. Things that I didn't need anymore and things I should never have bought in the first place. I'm old enough to remember Fibber McGee's closet and it wasn't funny anymore. I haven't always had so much. I never did without anything I needed growing up, but I definitely didn't have everything I wanted. I remember how happy I was when I did get something new, and I had to want something badly before I would spend my babysitting money.

My grandmother would not be proud of me. Waste and excess were sin in her Bible. All these years later I can still hear her admonishment to me when I left the hot water running to rinse dishes, "I can tell you never carried water in a bucket." She didn't even waste water filling the sink when she washed dishes. She made dishwater in a large pan or bowl waiting to be washed, and when she finished, used it to water the flowers around the back door. She never understood the concept of paper towels. Why would anyone use something once and throw it away?

Grandma saved everything to use again. After her visits with me, my cabinet and closet doors would no longer close because they contained every empty jar, lid, rubber band, empty envelope, snippet of string, paper bag, and box that had found its way into the house during her visit. There was no need for a garbage disposal because every edible scrap of food was transformed into nutritious soup or became a handout for some stray cat or dog. No piece of clothing was ever discarded, but refurbished instead.

We Laughed At Her Funeral

My grandmother was recycling before the word existed and no amount of affluence would have changed her. Frequently I still hear her saying, "Use what you have before you buy more."

With all I have, in some ways, I have less. I have less time because I have to use and take care of all that I have. I have less peace of mind because I worry that something might happen to it, or that someone might steal it. I have less to give to others because I spent so much on myself. I have less satisfaction because I always want something else or something better. I have less pride because there are times when I am embarrassed by what I have accumulated. I can also hear my Heavenly Father say, "*Don't store up treasures on earth...instead store up your treasures in heaven, where moths and rust cannot destroy them, and thieves cannot break in and steal them. Your heart will always be where your treasure is*" *(Matthew 6:19-21, CEV).*

On second thought, maybe affluence was not the word I heard that evening. Maybe it was *allfullance*. If only our treasuries in heaven were as full and our hearts as overflowing.

Road To Success

Once upon a time I had a friend who cared about people. Mostly he cared about people's feelings. It was a becoming trait and won him the respect of many. My friend was proud of his family and loved them very much. He dreamed of providing them with more and better, and with that in mind, he imagined what it might be like to set out to seek his fortune.

Along the way he befriended many who were seeking the same, but, alas, while he stopped often along the way to lend a hand or stepped aside for another, he noticed that those around him kept their eyes on the road ahead and moved steadily upward. Observing the rapid gain of these fellow travelers and being aware of his own interrupted progress, he resolved to follow more closely in their footsteps. First, he noted, they took no detours. So he stopped going out of his way to do for others. Once he thought he heard a friend calling him, but with his eyes fixed on the road to success as he had learned, he couldn't be sure. Next he noticed that the others didn't play along the way except among themselves and then only when it served a useful purpose. Reluctantly he began to turn down invitations from his friends until, after a while, there were none. Then he noticed these successful ones never rested, even on the Sabbath. Therefore, with a pang of regret, he resigned from his church responsibilities. Sometimes

We Laughed At Her Funeral

his children coaxed him to play, but he'd learned from the others to leave that to his wife and consoled himself instead with visions of the things he would buy for them. My friend often heard his wife crying, which was a sound new to him. "Women just do that," the other travelers told him, and so he learned to ignore her. Time became his most valuable commodity, and he shared it with only those who could offer something of value in return. Once he realized the risk in trusting others, he was able to curb that dangerous habit, and in its place developed a selfish streak. Because he was a fast learner and practiced all that he was taught his fortune grew rapidly.

After a while, my friend grew weary. With the realization that he missed his family and longed for the simple pleasures of times past, he decided to drop out of the race. When he returned home he found his house cold and empty. His wife had gone to live with someone else and wasn't crying anymore. His children were scattered, each seeking in what seemed to him like strange places for something they remembered vaguely from their past. He coaxed them to talk to him, but they were too busy. He was lonely and sometimes sat on the sidelines and called out to his friends still running the race, but they had their eyes on the road to success and didn't stop.

In his despair, he cried aloud.

"What are you going on about?" his wife asked. "What of your fortune?"

Suddenly my friend's eyes were open wide, he was no longer dreaming and he knew exactly where his fortune was. His fortune was under his own roof.

> *"No one can serve two masters. The person will hate one master and love the other, or will follow one master and refuse to follow the other. You cannot serve both God and worldly riches" (Matthew 6:24, TISB).*

Was My Prayer Answered?

If there is one command God gave that I have obeyed it is, "Pray without ceasing."

I have always prayed. I started at a young age and I'm sure it was mostly asking. I knew nothing about form or content or the Model Prayer. I just knew I needed to talk to someone and God was always available. I had read in the Bible that one should enter into the closet to pray and so I did. I spent so much time in the closet that my parents would probably have had me analyzed if we hadn't been so poor.

Another thing I did back then was try to make bargains with God. I must have learned that from my brothers. Although I always knew that I was loved, that was the only thing I knew for sure. Our home life was chaotic and no two days were ever the same. Aware that alcohol was often the source of the trouble and since I had no other resource, I talked my problems over with God. I remember one "deal" in particular. If God would prevent Daddy from stopping off for a drink after work, I would read my Bible every day. I did my part, but it was thirty-five years before Dad's health forced him to break the habit completely. In the meantime, I had become quite familiar with my Bible. I ask you, did God honor our deal?

My brother, being older and male, felt it was his duty to torment me and often did so by starting debates with me regarding what I believed. I prayed hard and often for him, interpreting his teasing as unbelief. It was many years later that he shared with me his long time deep faith. Was that an answer to my prayer?

I have never run out of loved ones to worry about. Two young members of our extended family experienced one hardship after another and were perpetually unhappy. Out of my reach, but not my concern, I continued to pray for them even when it appeared to be in vain. After they were grown and had lost both parents they moved back close, and it was to me they came for counseling and advice. Was God using me to answer my own prayers?

After my husband and I had been married for a few years, we found the perfect house for sale. I can still remember how badly I wanted that house and how I prayed and prayed. While we were trying to get together the down payment, someone else bought the dream house. Soon afterward another house became available. A larger house in a better location, and it was more affordable. The time was right and we were prepared to make the purchase. I ask you, were my prayers answered?

My daughter copied an idea from Kathryn Marshall's writings and wrote a description of the girl she prayed her son would someday marry. Then she folded it and tucked it away privately in her Bible. Many young women came and went during the following years, but he didn't choose a wife until the "girl in the Bible" came into his life. Did God answer her prayer or was it just a coincidence? If so, it was a divine coincidence.

All my prayers have not had delayed responses. Often God performs miracles before my eyes and ears in response to my silent pleas. I often write my prayers in a journal and later make notes in the margins telling how God answered. I can flip back through the journal pages when I need reassurance and am reminded how God works. There have been times in my life when I could not form the words to pray, and God read my thoughts, and times when I pleaded for the wrong thing and God edited the prayer. Other times He simply made me wait.

I have learned a lot about prayer since I first started praying. While a peaceful place and a humble position enhance my prayers, I no longer need to pray in the closet. My heart is His altar and I can approach him there wherever I am. There is no wrong place, stance, or form. I have learned to pray spontaneously for forgiveness, for guidance, for the right word to speak, and especially to give thanks. I talk to God about everything. A parking place when I really need one, an unknown person when I hear an ambulance in the distance, or when I see a child with tears. When I don't know what to say next or I feel myself losing control, I pray. A beautiful sky or a fragrant flower prompts me to give thanks. God is as close to me as a thought at all times, and when He's that close and I know it, it affects the way I behave, too. Even though I probably still pray asking for more than I should, my prayers now include more praise and more thanksgiving, but sometimes I just want to talk things over with God.

I have never found a scripture that says, "Give thanks

without ceasing," but I often think of a story, written by a missionary, about visiting with an old man who was blind, ill, poor, and completely dependent on the goodness of others. When the missionary asked the man if he could pray with him, the poor soul's reply was, "Yes, but let it be mostly thanksgiving."

"For the eyes of the Lord are over the righteous, and His ears are attentive to their prayer" (1 Peter 3:12).

The Fabric of Faith

You may be surprised to know that I speak three languages. I'm still struggling with English, but I have no trouble communicating with my flowers and I have a fabric stash that calls out to me regularly. Just last week I was deadheading some violets that had almost stopped blooming when I noticed the stems had bent way over so the tiny seed pods at the tip ends were close to the dirt in a position to best plant next season's flowers.

One of the little plants said to me, "I see changes in you also. I believe that you're closer to the ground than you used to be, and you don't stand as erect as you once did. I notice your fingers aren't as quick and nimble on the clippers, either. You don't visit the garden nearly as often as you used to, and you're much slower getting up and down."

The once bright and fragrant little blossom, now limp and dull and very irritating, continued, "I'll soon have completed my reason for being. The Master Landscaper is satisfied with me. How about you?"

I didn't have a smug answer, but I did plop down in the nearby swing and seriously wonder if I were cooperating with my Maker.

Later in the week, I was sorting and rearranging my sewing area when one after another of my unfinished projects started to haunt me. Usually when I sorted

The Fabric of Faith

through my storage, my mind danced and sang with ideas and inspiration. That day I just faced a small mountain of carefully selected, carefully folded, and neatly packaged projects, each in some stage of incompletion. I love fabric. I love to look at it, to feel it, and to imagine what it will become. I have favorites, of course, and others that I avoid. Some types are a real pleasure to sew with, some types are a challenge, and a few can really try my patience. Like flowers, fabric talks to me and tells me what it dreams of becoming.

While I was sorting through the stacks, a pretty piece of linen caught my eye. Then I heard Lovely Linen whisper, "I was going to be a suit, but I wrinkle easily and wasn't used."

"Like people, all fabric isn't designed for the same purpose," I replied. "Here beside you is Elegant Silk, a beautiful fabric to look at and to touch, but one that requires very careful laundering. The Organza has been stuck away here only because little girls don't wear pinafores anymore. Knits are practical and easy to care for, but they are so out of style right now. Rayon is a real partygoer until it starts to ravel, and Cotton is everyone's favorite because it's so durable, comfortable, and colorful. Colorful that is, until it fades."

Not satisfied with what I thought was a good answer, Lovely Linen's next question was, "Did you dream of becoming something that hasn't happened?"

I did know the answer to that question. "Yes, I've dreamed of many things that didn't happen, Lovely Linen."

I want to be good at whatever I do. I like to make a good grade, a good meal, a good impression. When I sew, I'm not happy unless the seams are straight, the buttonholes are all the same size, and the wrong side is as neat as the right side. For that reason, I don't attempt anything I know I can't do well. I can't throw or catch a ball, so I don't play sports. I can't carry a tune, so I don't sing solos–even in the shower. I don't argue much, not because I don't want to, but because I'm not well equipped. Maybe most importantly, I don't submit manuscripts for publication for fear of receiving rejections.

Some of my dreams haven't come true, Lovely Linen, not because I'm not good enough, but because I *think* I'm not. I'm sure there are plans God has made for me that I have not had the faith to attempt. No, Little Violet, I can't say with your confidence that the Master is yet satisfied with me. As you so wisely observed, my season is getting short, but I pray there is still time for me to gather up His plans and create a beautiful coat of many colors that will satisfy Him.

When God is the designer how can we fail?

"For we are God's workmanship, created in Christ Jesus to do good works, which God prepared in advance for us to do" (Ephesians 2:10, NIV).

Stop, Look, and Listen

I'm sure through the years I have forgotten many very important happenings. What puzzles me is why I remember the particular things I do. Why, for instance, after so many years do I remember vividly a poster from kindergarten? I can still clearly visualize the smiling police officer in his blue uniform and hat, a whistle on a lanyard in one hand, and his other hand held out in front of him, palm forward. On the poster in large letters were the words, "Stop! Look! Listen!"

The purpose of that visual aid was to attract the attention of little children, to linger in their minds and to remind them how to safely cross the street. Years later the same three words became important when I was learning to drive. Lately that message has again been rolling around in my head, and this time God has become the virtual police officer and the slogan changed to, "Stop what you're doing, look around, and listen."

I was thinking about that recently when a traffic light stopped me. I didn't really have time to stop, but the law says I have to when the light is red. So while I waited, I looked around. What I saw was an old man walking on the side of the road. He was very poorly dressed in worn, dirty clothes, and the weight of the sack on his shoulder bent him over. He pulled one foot in front of the other as he walked as if each one weighed more than he could lift.

I felt my heart go out to him. I wondered where he was going and where he would sleep that night. While I was watching the old man, I heard a honk from the car behind me letting me know the light had changed. I drove on and he kept walking, but I couldn't stop thinking about him. What could have happened to cause some mother's dear little boy to grow up to be a hopeless, helpless wanderer? What if he were one of mine? I looked, I saw beyond myself, and I prayed.

I like to get up early in the morning, and I usually have a list of things to do. This particular day I had planned to run errands and spray the roses in my garden, but it was raining. More than that; it was storming, and in the still-dark sky, each lightening strike gave an eerie, strange, almost beautiful look to the ordinary. The thunder cracked, rumbled, and roared in that early morning darkness with such a sound of authority that it might have been God clearing His throat. As the big sounds of the storm rolled on and on into the distance with a low echoing rumble, just outside my window I could hear the quiet, gentle spattering of raindrops as they joined others in the puddles already collecting. I saw the lights of a car in the dark and heard its tires pick up and throw the puddles into solid sheets of water. From inside I listened to the refreshing, restoring rain's rhythmic beat. I forgot about the errands, about spraying roses, and I thought about God, and His power and His gentleness. I'm glad I didn't miss His spectacular waterworks that morning because I took time to stop, look, and listen.

Stop, Look, and Listen

On my way to an appointment and with no time to spare, I stopped at my son's house to leave a package. There was a new bunny in their family and despite my rush, a little coaxing resulted in my waiting "just a minute" so I could meet him. How do you describe the feeling that comes from having a sweet, soft bunny fall asleep in your lap, and a grandson curled up close beside you? Stopping that day made me late... and very happy.

In the middle of a busy day my friend called to talk. I was impatient to end the conversation and get back to what I was doing, when I heard a tremor in her voice and a quiet sob. Underneath what sounded to me like idle chatter, she was trying to hide a heart-breaking concern. I had no answer to give her, but I did have time to stop and listen with my heart.

Now, I not only wonder what happenings I have forgotten, but how many I have missed. How much beauty and how many miracles have I left unseen? How much music has escaped my hearing and how many calls for help? How many opportunities have I overlooked because I didn't stop, look, and listen?

A framed piece of embroidery, made for me by a friend, hangs over my desk. It says, "Taking time for Love is more important than getting things accomplished." In my keepsake box, a note from my son reminds me, "We need to see the things around us anew, move beyond the obvious and see in that which is, that which could be."

"Blessed are your eyes, for they see: and your ears, for they hear" (Matthew 13:16).

We Laughed At Her Funeral

"Turn my eyes away from worthless things; renew my life according to your word" (Psalm 119:37, NIV).

Spiritual Computerish

Several years ago, when the school where I was teaching began using computers I decided once and for all that I wanted no part of them. I did want my job however, so when I was dragged screaming and struggling to the trough of modern technology, I drank up. It turned out to be a lot like eating vegetables; to my surprise, I liked it.

About the same time that I was being converted from typewriter to computer, I was told that in the near future anyone who didn't know at least the basics about computers would be considered illiterate. Since I didn't want to be so labeled, I decided to home school myself in computerish. For a textbook I chose the Bible and selected the story in *Luke 18:9-14,* where the prayer of a Pharisee is recorded. It isn't a prayer that you or I would have prayed, of course, but some of it did sound a bit familiar. Why wouldn't it? Some of those thoughts had, at some time, been recorded on my disc.

My disc? "Disc" was the first vocabulary word I learned in computerish. It is the part of the computer where information is stored and where it remains until it is deleted or changed. Even if you don't have a computer, you have a disc. You may never know what is on my disc, and I may never know what is on your disc, but there is One who does. According to my textbook, God can read our discs. It says, *"I know the things that come into your mind, every one of them" (Ezekiel 11:5b).*

Now, I am a nice person, so why would I have any of that Pharisee's kind of thinking on my disc? Because my *program* is *user friendly*. A *program* makes a computer work in a certain way. There are highly technical programs that only the very skilled understand, and there are simple programs that even I can work. An easy-to-operate program is called *user friendly*. Whether they are user friendly or technical, everyone wants to write on my disc. Everyone wants to influence the way I think and behave and spend my money, and no one more than Satan. I turned in my textbook and read, *"Be self controlled and alert. Your enemy the devil prowls around like a roaring lion looking for someone to devour" (Peter 5:8, NIV).*

Sometimes I allow Satan to program my thinking, and sometimes he does it when I'm not even aware. How does he do that? Satan is highly skilled in *computer piracy*. That is when someone messes around with someone else's information. Such as when a student gets into the school's computer system and changes his grades, or a depositor gets into the bank's system and increases his balance, or one business successfully erases the records of another. Satan loves nothing better than to confuse my thinking in this way. What can I do to prevent that happening? I can write protect myself. When a disc is *write protected* nothing can be added, changed, or deleted without permission. It is sealed. There are directions in my textbook for doing this, *"Be careful what you think, because your thoughts run your life" (Proverbs 4:23, TISB)*, and *"Use every piece of God's armor to resist the enemy whenever he attacks..." (Ephesians 6:13-18, TLB)*.

I eventually mastered basic computerish, and more importantly I learned that with the same basics I could better live my life by allowing only my Heavenly Father to program my disc and to write protect myself from Satan's interference. I can even replace any of the Pharisee's prayer that might be on my disc with that of the tax collector's: *"God have mercy on me, sinner that I am" (Luke 18:13, NIV)*.

Now that I understand basic computerish, my prayer is, *"Let the words of my mouth and the meditations [on my disk] be acceptable in your sight, Oh Lord, my strength and my Redeemer" (Psalms 19:14)*.

LOVE: THE REAL THING

With apologies to Elizabeth Barrett Browning, I have had a phrase stuck in my head for a while. "What do I love? Let me count the things." I love football. I love Mom. I love ice cream. I love God. I just love your new coat, the nice weather, and my new neighbors. I really love attending Bible study and going to the beach. On and on it goes. . .

Love. Now there is a busy word! Can you think of any other used as often or with as many definitions? In Biblical days there were three different words for love, each with a different meaning. Today we use one word to cover the whole gamut, leaving the listener to determine what kind of love we intended and to define how much. I guess it is the same principal as beauty being in the eye of the beholder or understanding being in the ear of the listener. You select the meaning it has for you.

I decided to do a little checking and found more than 500 quotes containing the word "*love*" in the *Oxford Dictionary of Quotations*. Without even looking I knew the Bible used the word far more times than I could count. The piano bench contained two songbooks with dozens of love songs, and I found six books dedicated to the topic in only one of my bookcases. Everyday even more songs, books, plays, and poems appear on the subject. I found references to puppy love, brotherly love, platonic love, spiritual love, romantic love, and self-love, to name a few. It was obvious that parents give it, children feel it, and newlyweds can live on it. Older folks understand it, and everyone knows that there's no such thing as too much of it. In hardly any time at all and with very little effort, I found myself surrounded in love.

Since the advent of cell phones, I seem to be an ear-witness to many phone conversations in public not intended for me. Also quite without intention, I have observed a new trend of ending those phone conversations with the phrase, "love you," in place of "good-bye." I heard that three times just today. I think it's nice, if it's sincere. If love makes the world go 'round, as someone said, and if we all love as much as we proclaim, one would think our globe would be spinning with joy. Obviously, it is not. With so much love in the air, why isn't the world a happier place? Do we not understand the meaning of the word, or have we altered the definition?

Chapter 13 of *I Corinthians* describes what love requires of us. It tells us to be patient and kind, not to be selfish, not to brag, or to be proud. We should not be rude, self-seeking, quick-tempered, or carry grudges. Our joy should come from good things and not evil. It tells us to trust, have hope, and be strong, and that true love doesn't come and go. Love is not selective. "*You shall love the Lord your God with all your heart, and with all your soul, and with all your strength, and with all your mind; and love your neighbor as yourself*" *(Luke 10:27).*

Love is a very popular word and a very popular topic.

Love is an easy word to say, but loving requires much more. How wonderful to be told, "I love you," by someone who knows exactly what the word means!

And then there is that *other* word. . . don't you just *hate* philosophical people?

Does It Matter?

It has taken me a long time to learn some of the simplest things…like what matters, and what does not, and what is important enough to need my attention and what is not worth the grief I allow it to generate. A black snake likes to camp out in the vicinity of my back step. I do not like that a bit, and I do not think the snake likes me any better, because the first of us to spy the other quickly takes off in the opposite direction. Even though I do not like being surprised by his presence, I know that his being around doesn't really matter.

There is currently a dead limb dangling from a large oak tree over my patio. It is eventually going to turn loose without warning and drop with some force. It could fall harmlessly, or it could hit someone. It does matter. It needs attention.

One of our daughters was born and still is, quite *spirited*. That was the term we chose to describe her rather than hardheaded, strong-willed, stubborn, determined, or a few other of Dr. Spock's labels. Even though this trait has served her well as an adult, she was sometimes a challenge as a child. From our first encounter with her in the hospital, peeking out of a soft pink blanket and as sweet and pretty as a picture, she was determined to have the last word. From that day, in my attempt to reign over her, we battled daily. I fussed, scolded, and corrected her endlessly. Needless to say, neither of us was very happy. An older and very wise friend gave me the advice that turned things around. He said, "Some things matter, and some things don't. What you see you must deal with, but what you don't see, you don't have to do anything about. The trick is to not see the things that don't matter and only see those that do." It worked. When I did see something I had to deal with, it took on more importance than when I overlooked nothing and was harping about everything. We both benefited.

I know it is of little interest to others, all these years later, how I disciplined my child, but if you are wondering where this is going, I will tell you. The same thing works in my relationships with others. Some things matter, some things don't. When I overlook unimportant issues and concentrate on things that do matter, it helps me to avoid getting so easily upset, angry, or disappointed. It allows me to be less critical, less judgmental, and much kinder. I notice that others *listen more* when I *say less*. It also allows me to give more attention to real problems instead of fretting over trivia.

Sometimes, however, I have difficulty in separating the two. Just this week I was very upset and embarrassed when a good friend stopped by unexpectedly while passing through town. If only she had called first! Everything in my house was in disarray, I had nothing prepared to offer for refreshment, and I had not even combed my hair that morning. After a few minutes of hugging and sharing though, I forgot my embarrassment and had a

Does It Matter?

wonderful visit. What really mattered was not me or my untidy house, but that she wanted to see me. Other times I mistake disappointment for a dilemma–like a rained-out picnic, a poor test grade, someone's careless remark, a missed opportunity, or cakes that fall.

Are you angry about something? Did someone hurt your feelings? Are you perplexed or anxious? Are you trading peace of mind for worry when it is not necessary? Ask yourself if it really matters, or how important it really is. The good news may be that it does not matter. Otherwise, remember that when it is something you cannot overlook, we have access to the wisest of all Friends–One who sees everything and does not make mistakes.

> *"The Lord himself goes before you and will be with you; he will never leave you nor forsake you. Do not be afraid; do not be discouraged" (Deuteronomy 31:8).*

A Heavenly View

A fleeting fascination with Harry Potter and an appreciation for *The Lion, the Witch and the Wardrobe* are about the extent of my interest in science fiction, which makes me wonder why this puzzling thought is rattling around in my mind lately. If an alien reporter was dispatched to Earth for a few days with an assignment to write a brief description of life here, as it appeared to him, what do you suppose he would see? How do you think we would be described…physically, mentally, and spiritually?

As far as appearance is concerned, I can safely say that very little shocks or surprises me anymore. Recently we took a trip to an entertainment park, and I can think of no other place where the reporter could have gotten a better random look at people of every age, race, or circumstance. Some we saw in the park were healthy and robust specimens, many were overweight, while others were skinny and sickly. We saw hair as colorful as flowers, and lines and drawings on the arms and legs of many of the people. All ages were represented from the very old and frail being pushed in wheelchairs, to newborns sleeping in strollers. There were those in the crowd who were considerate and polite and others who pushed, shoved, and used abusive language. I am at a total loss as to how to describe the way people were dressed–from meticulous to scandalous. How

A Heavenly View

can I explain the number walking around with devices pressed to their heads or with an antenna of some type attached to their ear? It frightens me to imagine how we would be portrayed.

I'm sure it would be obvious at once to any alien that we are mental giants. One look around at the technology that we have developed would prove that. However, what would our politics, our wars, our many prisons and rehabilitation centers, and our large number of unsolved social problems say about our intellect and mentality?

Describing us from a spiritual viewpoint could be the most difficult part of all for an alien. While we all call ourselves "believers" we cannot even agree on what to believe. Recently I came upon a debate of interest on the internet between two people concerning a current moral issue now in the news. One of the writers quoted a scripture from the Bible in defense of her argument, and the other flatly discredited the Bible as being unauthentic.

Following this there were pages and pages of comments added by other readers stating their strong feelings about God and the Bible one way or the other. Considering my own personal convictions, I was sick at heart after reading those comments and realizing that more of the writers agreed with the doubter than those who defended God and the divinity of the Bible. I was shocked at the number of people who claimed no faith at all. What would that stranger to our planet assume from reading our books, watching our television shows and movies, or listening to the lyrics of our popular music? He might be confused when he observed that we associated our Savior's birth with flying reindeer and His death with colored eggs and chocolate bunnies. Even though I refuse to believe that doubters are in the majority, everything considered, an alien might get that impression.

Actually, I am not concerned at all about what an alien might see or think about us, but I know for sure that there is One among us who does see us as we really are, and who is keeping records. I know too, regardless of all other theories and arguments to the contrary, that His Holy Bible instructs us how to live and how to ensure our salvation.

I wonder how God would describe us from His view.

"For the word of God is living and active. Sharper than any double-edged sword, it judges the thoughts and attitudes of the heart. Nothing in all creation is hidden from God's sight. Everything is uncovered and laid bare before the eyes of him to whom we must give account" (Hebrews 4:12-13 NIV).

For God So Loved the World

When I was five, I went to live with my grandmother temporarily. Of course when I was five, I didn't understand about temporary. I just remember one adventuresome day at a time, and I remember her.

My grandmother was old when I was five. Her hair was gray. The skin on her hands was thin and shiny and blue veins lay on top off them. Her fingers never straightened out completely, but she could wring clothes so tightly I could hear the threads break. It didn't matter that Grandmother was old; she was always up before Grandpa or me. She cooked mostly on the wood stove on the back porch so the kitchen where we ate and where the new gas stove was would stay cooler.

My grandmother didn't go to work, but people brought her work. She washed their clothes in a big tub of hot water heated on the wood stove. After they had washed, she put them through a wringer into the tub of rinse water where she had put the bluing to make them white. It looked like fun poking the clothes through the wringer, but she would never let me do it. She just pointed to the scar under her arm to remind me of the time when she got her arm caught in one. It made me want to cry when I thought how badly it must have hurt her. That was not the same arm that had the strawberry birthmark on it, though. I always forgot that red mark was on her arm and neck until someone asked her about it. Most of the time she made up something to tell them and then she would look at me and smile because we knew the truth; God put that mark on her special, and it didn't matter why. She told me that people would rather hear a sad story than the truth.

Sometimes I buried my face in the clean clothes drying on the line. By then they smelled more like fresh air and sunshine than the homemade lye soap that made my nose burn. I especially liked the sound of the sheets snapping in the wind. When the clothes were dry Grandmother dampened them again with water from a pop bottle and rolled them up tightly to iron the next day.

In the Spring Grandmother planted tomato seeds in shallow wooden boxes she called flats. When they grew tall enough, people came to buy them. She showed me a place in the flower border where weeds that looked like tomato plants grew, and she let me pretend I was selling plants too. I helped Grandmother a lot with her work. Every day I swept the sidewalk in front of the house and picked the wilted pansy blooms in the flowerbeds. That was an important job because if I didn't keep them picked, they stopped blooming. I knew all the flowers by name and the iris were my favorites. I always wanted to pick them, but Grandmother said we should leave them outside for everyone to enjoy.

For God So Loved the World

The upstairs bedrooms at Grandmother's house were scary at night, especially when a small light appeared on the wall near the ceiling and moved all around the room like a ghost, then disappeared. Grandmother wasn't scared though, she said it was only lights from passing cars, but she never made me sleep up there alone.

I could tell where I was at Grandmother's house with my eyes closed if my nose was working. The kitchen was the best place of all because something was always cooking or baking there. It made me hungry just to come inside unless I came in through the porch door. That is where Grandpa's brass spittoon was. The cellar was my least favorite place. The door to the cellar was in the kitchen and when I opened it all I could see at the bottom of the steep steps was black, and the air down there was musty like wet dirt and apples.

Grandmother could not drive so we walked wherever we went. I liked to walk with Grandmother because we stopped a lot and sat on the porches of one or another of the other old people in the neighborhood. Sometimes they asked me to say a piece and when I did, they laughed and clapped, and Grandmother looked so proud. On Sunday we walked to church. The preaching lasted a long time, and I usually went to sleep after I got tired of writing with the pencil she kept in her purse. I think Grandmother did too.

In the evenings when all her work was done, and Grandpa had gone to bed, we played games; mostly dominoes. Sometimes she told me stories about when she was young. I liked the stories, but I don't know why because they were mostly sad. Other times they were about funny things that happened at the Poor Farm where she worked, or about the babies she helped the old country doctor deliver. I knew more about having babies than any of my friends.

Nights were cozy there. When it was cold, Grandmother put a brick on the stove early in the evening and at bedtime she wrapped it in old newspapers and a towel and put it in my bed to keep my feet warm. If I were awake at night, I could hear the clock in the kitchen bonging the time. I loved the sound of it, especially at night.

I was happy at Grandmother's house. She was never cross with me, only with Grandpa. But she didn't like it when I slammed the screen door, or when I snuffed, or when I said "yeah" instead of "yes." It was almost fun to be sick at her house because she cooked the things that I liked best and gave me the catalog to cut paper dolls from. When I got homesick, she put me on the train and told the conductor to be sure I got off at the right stop. Sometimes I cried when it was time to go back, but I don't know why. What could have been better than Grandmother's house?

By the time my first grandchild, Jonathan, was five, his grandmother (me) was also old. As it happens, her hair is gray too, but her skin isn't thin and shiny; it's tanned and spotted. She doesn't have blue veins on her hands, but they are big and bulging behind her knees. His grandmother also gets up early, but she cooks breakfast in the microwave. She doesn't wash clothes in a tub or iron them at all. She doesn't even have a clothesline. When his grandmother goes to her air-conditioned office to work, she wears her good clothes and drives her own car.

Jonathan's grandmother doesn't grow tomato plants, just a strawberry plant that only he can eat the berries from, and all kinds of flowers that she lets him pick and take to his mother. There are no attics in his grandmother's house, no buildings full of old fashioned equipment or a chicken house where he can gather eggs. But he can climb to the top of her magnolia tree, and there is a hidden place between the shrubbery and fence that only he knows about. At her house there are shelves and drawers full of old things that he is allowed to play with if he is careful, and his mother's books are in the bookcase with writing inside where she practiced her name when she was five.

Jonathan gets to spend the night at his grandmother's more often than the others because he is the oldest. Her house is not big or old or dark and doesn't make strange noises at night, but she lets him leave a light on anyway. There is a very old clock in his grandmother's kitchen that bongs in the night, and she told him that if he marries the right girl, she will give it to him.

Jonathan's grandmother doesn't tell sad stories, but sometimes she is funny. She forgets and calls him by his brother's name and tells the same things over and over. At her house he is allowed to do things he doesn't do at home. It is okay if he drips water off his elbows onto to kitchen floor when he helps her with the dishes or if he spills a little pancake batter when he is making them into doughnut shapes to surprise Granddaddy. His grandmother gives him cookies between meals and doesn't care if he goes barefoot or plays in the hose with his clothes on. She almost never fusses at him and believes him when he tells her about the panthers and other wild animals that he has seen from the magnolia tree.

A lot has changed over the years, but love has not. At five Jonathan did not yet realize how much his grandmother loved him, and she has only begun to understand how much her grandmother loved her when she was five.

Which of us can ever comprehend how much God loves each one of us?

> *"For God so loved the world that He gave his only begotten Son, that whosoever believeth in him should not perish, but have everlasting life" (John 3:16).*

It's Just A Little Thing

I have heard it said that bigger isn't always better, but I am thinking that neither is a little thing always less. I guess everyone has had an ant bite at some time. Those little jaws can chomp down hard, and sting like a dragon's tongue. A few ant bites can make one sick. A spider can kill. A mosquito can chase away a grown man. A splinter can make a thumb useless, and the flame of a candle can burn down a city. Think about all the pain and damage that can be caused by just a little thing.

In my case, those little things are sometimes just words. A long time ago, but after I was old enough to know better, I wrote on the back of a classmate's school picture: "She hangs around with me a lot, but I don't like her much." I don't remember now why I wrote that, but the reason I remember doing it is because she later picked up the picture and read what I had written. Can you imagine how inadequate I was in my attempt to explain? Lasting harm? I don't know, but even after all these years I still remember her reaction and how ashamed I felt.

Who hasn't said something unkind or hurtful about another only to discover them standing within hearing distance, or repeated some juicy gossip about another that turned out to be untrue? How many promises to not tell another soul have slipped out? How many encouraging words have been left unsaid? Even though I never intentionally lie about things, I am sometimes guilty of knowingly leaving a false impression, just by keeping quiet when I should speak. Come to think about it, even though I have never carried a weapon, I have the potential to be very dangerous. I can't help but wonder how many I have carelessly wounded. What makes me do this?

Anger is the culprit that sometimes sets my tongue free to say things which I would not ordinarily say. Impatience is often the prompter of unkind words that would be better left unsaid. Pride thinks it must defend me when I look bad or to build me up in the eyes of others. Competition urges me to put others down so I can be lifted up. I have a defensive guard that is always present with appropriate words if I feel threatened. Lest I fail to give credit where it is due, the devil sometimes puts words in my mouth when I am off guard.

Even though hurting others with words is often done carelessly or without intent, there is no taking them back. I can swat the mosquito or put a band aid on the bite, but all the regret I can muster cannot retrieve words. Once a feather pillow is opened in the wind, there is no way to stop the spread of the little feathers. With that in mind, and with that much power and air space, consider the potential our words have for doing good instead of harm. Just a little thing spoken sincerely at the right moment can open the door to a multitude of miracles.

A word of praise encourages, a few words of appreciation inspire, a word of empathy comforts, a soft answer can derail a quarrel. On and on it goes. The scriptures tell us numerous times what an influence our words have on others. The choice is ours; cruel and damaging, or warm and healing, words are powerful. Words paint mental pictures, ugly or beautiful. Words reveal our hearts, pure or deceitful. Strangers sometimes form their first opinion of us based on just our choice of words. My mother often reminded me that my conversation was my advertisement, or better yet, the scripture tells us that it is from the heart that the mouth speaks.

I pray that by taking time to listen to what I am saying I can avoid hurting others, starting rumors, or spreading gossip, and that by being more attuned to the needs and feelings of others I can be a better ambassador for God even when it is just a little thing.

> *"With the tongue we praise our Lord and Father, and with it we curse men, who have been made in God's likeness. Out of the same mouth come praise and cursing. My brothers, this should not be. Can both fresh water and saltwater flow from the same spring? My brothers, can a fig tree bear olives or a grapevine bear figs?" (James 3:9-12).*

My Clock Will Not Run Backwards

My hundred-year-old clock will not run backwards. Today I took it off the kitchen shelf, where it has been for more than forty years, and packed it in a box to be taken to a shop for repair. Not because it won't run backwards but because it has stopped chiming on the hour; which can be fixed, I am told. It has only been packed up twice before that I know about. How often I wish I could turn it back in time.

When I was five years old, I temporarily went to live with my grandmother for reasons I didn't understand at the time any more than I understood "temporarily." I was happy living there and have a book-long list of happy memories. My grandmother's gift was that of being a caregiver, and I was but one of her benefactors. She lived in a very big, very old house with attics upstairs and a basement that smelled like damp dirt and apples. The house also smelled of bread baking and pies and the best waffles ever (before or since).

She made me dresses from flour sacks always a little too big, so I had room to grow, and they were pretty (even though nothing ever fit until it was worn out). On Sundays we went to church and Grandma tied a few coins in the corner of a handkerchief for me so I would not lose

My Clock Will Not Run Backwards

them. She tied them so tightly I had to have help getting the coins out to put in the collection plate, but I didn't lose them! She put a pencil and paper in her purse so I could draw when I got tired of listening to the sermon. She usually napped while I was drawing.

We walked everywhere we went because Grandpa liked to keep the car in the garage where it would not get dirty. On the way to town, we often stopped along the way and visited on the porches of other old people. Everyone was old then, as I remember now.

I started to school while I was living there with Grandma, and she saved the papers I brought home. I have them still with my first attempts at writing my name. I helped her gather black walnuts that stained my fingers from under a big tree. I can still remember the smell of them stored in the shed. The old clock was on a shelf in the kitchen over the sink and chimed on the hour and on the half-hour every day and all during the night. I especially loved the soothing sound of the chimes in the night, and I still do. After a while I returned home to my family, and a few years later we moved, this time a long distance from my grandmother. I grew up and she grew old.

Through the years we visited; I at her house, she at mine. She continued to seek every opportunity she could to take care of me and do things for me, just as she had when I was a child. On my last visit at her house, she quietly took the old clock off its shelf and carefully packed it into a box for me to bring home. It was the one thing of all she possessed that I wanted most, and I had not even asked. I was so happy to be the one given the clock, and I had every intention of finding the perfect place for it, preferably in the kitchen, but in my new home it just didn't fit in with my carefully coordinated decorating scheme. After a while it was boxed up once again and moved from place to place and eventually to the attic.

Grandma made one more trip to Florida to visit me after that. She looked around in vain for the clock, which was nowhere in sight, but never asked. I couldn't find words to express my shame, and because no excuse of mine would have been credible, the moment passed with no questions asked and no explanations given. Even as I write this so many years later, I can still feel the hurt–hers and mine.

Immediately after her visit I got the clock down, had it cleaned, had a shelf built in the kitchen and there it has been ever since. It chimes all during the day and the sound takes me back to being a child at her house. The chimes in the night remind me of those cold nights and her loving care. The old clock helps me to keep my values in perspective.

The clock won't run backwards. I wish it would because I would do things so differently. I have learned a lot through the years, while that old clock was ticking, about what is really important and what is not. I've learned how hurtful I can be unintentionally. I know too the potential impact of my decisions and my actions on others. Still, the clock won't run backwards.

> *"For wisdom will enter your heart, and knowledge will be pleasant to your soul. Discretion will protect*

you, and understanding will guard you" (Proverbs 2:9-11).

Only One Thing Is Needed

Ever notice how you can tell the seasons by the greeting card racks? The next day after Valentine's Day all the red and pink cards decorated with hearts and flowers have moved to the clearance racks along with candy in heart shaped boxes and the teddy bears wearing red bows. The card racks are suddenly green and shamrock-decked, and just today I noticed Easter was abloom in all the stores.

I love the Easter season, both the true celebration and the hoopla we have created around one of the two most important holy days of the Christian religion. Like Christmas, I can't deny the pleasure I get from the decorations, music, greeting cards, and fellowship that surround the holiday. My dilemma? Am I taking away from the sacredness of the occasion by adding all the frills? I hope not.

As a child Easter meant I would get a small Easter basket wrapped in cellophane with a hollow chocolate bunny standing in the center that I wanted to both save and to eat. It also meant that I would have something new to wear on Sunday; a dress or a new pair of shoes, or maybe both. It was the one Sunday of the year that we would all go to church as a family. Everyone went to church on Easter Sunday, and we knew we had to go early to get a seat. Some ladies wore corsages of real flowers and most wore a beautiful new hat. Even back then I knew the reason we got new clothes for Easter was because when Jesus came back from being dead. He was wearing all new clothes. It all had to do with the beauty that comes from new beginnings.

Easter was one of those occasions when we had a big dinner after church and lots of relatives came. Later in the day someone hid the eggs we had boiled and colored the day before and all the cousins hunted them, and the one who found the golden egg won a prize. One of the big kids always found it, of course. Thinking about it now, coloring the eggs was as much fun as hiding and finding them. We mixed food coloring with water and a little vinegar and made strange colors and a big mess.

I remember being told the legend of the colored eggs. The story tells about Simon of Cyrene, who placed his basket of eggs by the side of the road to help carry the Cross to Calvary and returned to find the eggs tinted the soft colors of the rainbow. It was supposedly the early Christians who were the first to color eggs and give them to their friends as a reminder that new life returns to nature at Easter time. Another legend was that a poor woman dyed eggs during a famine and hid them in a nest as an Easter gift for her children. Just as the children discovered the nest, a big rabbit leaped away. The story spread that the rabbit had brought the Easter eggs.

When I was old enough to be a part of the Youth group, we looked forward to getting up very early, meeting at the church, and taking a bus to a nearby town to attend the annual Easter Pageant. It was so authentic with all the costumes and props that it felt like I was a part of it. I especially remember watching Jesus struggle to carry the cross, but I got a little bored during the part about the Pharisees and the trial because I didn't understand it. By the time the Pageant was over I was tired from getting up so early and would sleep on the bus coming home. The next year, we were all anxious to go again just like we had never seen it before. The new clothes, colored eggs and Easter baskets continued to be an important part of the special day year after year.

I think it was after I had been married for a few years and had two little girls to get all dolled up for Easter, that my priorities went awry. I got so busy making each of them special dresses, finding hats and purses and little socks edged in lace to match, that I thought of little else. In addition to sewing, I spent hours making Easter baskets as big and special as I could imagine. It was not enough to just color the eggs with the children, but mine had to be beautifully decorated. Food had to be prepared for the next day's company dinner, including hot cross buns with a cross of icing on each one as a symbol of the cross, but seldom the traditional roast lamb (which I never really learned to prepare). The table had to be set with a fresh flower arrangement as a reminder that all the blooming bulbs and the budding trees were also signs of new life. Needless to say, Saturday night was hectic with last minute preparations.

By the time I had five granddaughters and five Easter

Only One Thing Is Needed

dresses to make, I was older and wiser but much slower. The last time I made that many dresses, I did not go to bed at all the night before Easter but was still putting in zippers and sleeves when the children's mothers brought them to our house on Easter morning to get dressed for Sunday school where they all arrived late, of course. I am a slow learner but smart enough to know that I was making a chore out of what was meant to be a blessing. I heard Jesus speaking words that I had heard before, "Martha, Martha... you are worried and upset about many things, but only one thing is needed..." This time, he was clearly speaking the words to me.

I still love the Easter decorations, the beautifully decorated eggs, the flowers, and food, and of course hiding eggs for grandchildren, but first and foremost I will spend time sitting at the foot of the cross.

> *"She had a sister called Mary, who sat at the Lord's feet listening to what he said. But Martha was distracted by all the preparations that had to be made... 'Martha, Martha,' the Lord answered, 'you are worried and upset about many things, but only one thing is needed... Mary has chosen what is better and it will not be taken away from her'"* (Luke 10:39-42).

The Gift of Giving

I had an unexpected opportunity last week to drop in for a short visit with two of my little great granddaughters. I keep a few small gifts stashed away for them so that when I see them, I can greet them with a surprise. This visit it was I who was surprised. The two year old met us at the door and quickly opened her gift, took a sweeping look, played briefly with the colorful wrapping, and then returned to what she had been doing. Later, while we were gathering our things to leave, her mother asked her if she had anything she wanted to give us. We both expected an obligatory hug and kiss, but instead she took off running into her room and came out carrying two sheets of paper covered in brightly colored finger-painted pictures. She proudly presented one to each of us and then stepped back, smiling from ear to ear and dancing in place excitedly, while she anticipated our response. Two years old and she already knew it was more fun to give than to get.

Giving is another of those words, like *love*, that is almost impossible to define. There are so many forms of giving and reasons for giving and attitudes about giving that they could fill a book and more. When I begin writing on a particular topic, like giving, I am often surprised by the things that my memory calls up from sometime past. So, it was with a story I can't seem to forget.

The Gift of Giving

As successful as he was, something appeared to be wrong in the life of a farmer who was a long-time faithful member of a small country church. While visiting the farmer one day, the pastor asked if there was a problem with the farm, and if so, if they could they pray together. The farmer appeared surprised and asked what made him ask that question. The pastor told him that he had noticed a change in his relationship with the church. His attendance had become irregular, his involvement had almost stopped, and that his dependable support of the church had been steadily declining. The farmer quickly reassured his friend and pastor that, indeed, just the opposite had occurred. The farm was now so successful that he was very busy, and with all the extra work to be done he hardly had time to attend church. As far as his giving was concerned, it had been much easier to give in the beginning, but that now a tithe would amount to a much larger sum than he could afford. The pastor replied, "How sad that is. Shall we pray that your profits will decline until you are once more able to resume your faithfulness to God?" Let us not forget from whom we received that which we have available to share.

I also recalled O. Henry's short story, *The Gift of the Magi*, which tells a beautiful tale of giving from the heart. When the young couple in the story found themselves unable to buy even simple Christmas gifts for one another, each secretly found a way to give to the other their very best. The wife cut and sold her beautiful hair in order to buy a fob for her husband's most treasured possession, his father's watch. Meanwhile, unknown to her, he had pawned his precious watch for money to buy combs for her beautiful hair. The reason for the gift is more valuable than the gift itself.

Because I wondered what the word "give" evoked in others, I asked a few people what first flashed into their mind when they considered giving. I emphasized that they be completely honest and not search for what they thought was the right answer. What I heard was, "money, help, gifts, time, and gratitude." When I asked, "To whom do you give?" the responses were "family, friends, church, missions, organizations, or the poor and needy."

The next question was, "Why?" What I heard was, "to help others, to support a cause, to make others happy, and compassion." Most gave gifts for special occasions, on holidays, or to show appreciation. Some said they gave out of gratitude for something they had been given, help they had received, or a kindness they had been shown. Others felt they had a duty or gave because they had more than they needed. For many the reason was simply that the scriptures clearly tell us we should. There were others who admitted that it was to ease their conscience, to impress others, to reduce excess, or because they believed God would reward them. Even tax advantages were mentioned. God knows our hearts. Unless our reason is acceptable to Him, our gift is not.

One person replied with his reason for not giving. His concern was for how the gift would be used. Again, I remembered having used that excuse myself and being

The Gift of Giving

told that when I gave something to another that it was no longer mine and that the responsibility for how it was used was then on the receiver and took nothing away from my gift of giving. To get a blessing from a gift, one must turn it loose, or it was never a gift in the first place.

The answer I liked most to the question, "Why do you give," was so simple; "Because it feels so good." When you think about it, what else does feel as good as giving, and even more so if given in secret, or to the undeserving, or when least expected? In addition, God knows just how to direct our gifts, and I suspect that He uses our from-the-heart giving like a boomerang to come back and bless us in ways we never imagined.

Last came the most difficult question of all; one that each of us must ask and answer ourselves, "What am I giving and why?"

> *"Remember this: Whoever sows sparingly will also reap sparingly, and whoever sows generously will also reap generously. Each man should give what he has decided in his heart to give, not reluctantly or under compulsion, for God loves a cheerful giver. And God is able to make all grace abound to you, so that in all things at all times, having all that you need, you will abound in every good work. As it is written: 'He has scattered abroad his gifts to the poor; his righteousness endures forever'" (2 Corinthians 9:6-9).*

Part Four

Poetry, Prayers, and Pondering

Envy the Season's Change

If only we could be more like the trees
Masters of permanence. Icons of strength and stability
Totally at peace. Unhurried and untroubled

Simple rules, which they would share, keep them strong
For trees know stress, as do we all; and yet they persevere
Trials come when times are dry
And, as with our own lives, they suffer when in need

The unexpected flood threatens to sweep them away
and leaves them clinging to their deepest foundations for support
How strange that with such common reminders
We do not heed their example
when troubles undermine the lives we lead

Even the mightiest tree emerges from a tiny sprout,
as delicate and fragile as our own simple beginnings
Feeding itself from God's blessings, which are ever-present and
abundant, it makes itself strong and stable from the sun, the
wind, and the rain.
Gifts we share, yet so often overlook

They live their lives with harmony
A balance of give and take
Without greed, they fill their need
Without selfishness, they in turn, support and nurture
While they sacrifice ambition for solitude and peace

Envy the Season's Change

who is to say which course is the more wise

Even in death they leave their mark
Their trunks linger for a while, a monument to themselves
And when they fall, their absence leaves a void
The branches of those nearby no longer twine with theirs
The wind and the water are altered by their absence
And those nearby are affected by their passing

A tree may fall from the forest unnoticed
A life may leave the world of billions
But the forest goes on, as our lives go on
Our legacy is judged by the depths of our roots

But the greatest lesson to be learned from the trees
is knowing when the seasons change

A season of cold, when you rely upon yourself
Calling on your reserves. Stripped of all pretense
Weathering the darkness that comes to us all
And waiting with hope for tomorrow's sun

A season of spring, when life returns
A promise fulfilled. A new beginning
A dawn awakening with promise and potential

Then summer's sun will come again
A time to work and to store
Living, breathing, and marking the days
until the wind becomes cooler,
and the shadows lengthen at close of day

But the most important lesson comes with autumn's leaves

We Laughed At Her Funeral

The season of surrender
For with the autumn's chill, the wise trees remember that
burdens must be released
Old things held dear must pass away
Leaves that have withered cannot bring strength
Old things once held dear must be cast away,
So new life has room to grow

They hold on tenaciously, though their work is done
But seasons will change, and so must the leaves
And so must we

The teachers surround us, and yet we pay no heed
They have been here longer than we,
taking the time for thought and reflection
Listen to the peace that they would teach
And envy the season's change.

J. Michael Grimes
Tennessee Mountain Solitude
August 2003

Love Knot

*Like a strong rope, a strong marriage is woven
of many strands. May yours be woven with:
A strand of gold for endurance,
A strand of silver for success,
A strand of silk for beauty,
A strand of ribbon for fun,
A strand of wool for warmth,
A strand of cotton for service,
A strand of crimson for forgiveness,
A strand of snow white for purity.*

*Let this strand of rope be a reminder to you both
that once the knot is tied you will be no longer
two, but one—each an extension of the other
and together stronger than either part.
Let the rope also remind you that the knot
once tied is not meant to be untied.*

A Marriage Prayer

Lord, take these two lives and tie them in a knot
Strong enough to hold fast for all their lives.
Tie a knot that will hold tightly on those occasions
When they are pulled in separate directions.

Tie a knot that will not unravel with the inevitable
Abrasion of word and deed.
Tie a knot strong enough to moor them securely
In the harbor of their love when all around them life is turbulent and stormy.
Tie them neither so tightly that they grow totally
Dependent on one another or loosely enough for
Either to become independent of the other.

Tie a knot that will stretch with patience
But never snap in anger.
Tie the knot in such a way that they may gather others in
But so that no one else can wriggle in.
Give them enough slack, Lord,
To allow them to venture along different paths
But not enough to let them
Lose sight of one another.

May they never use this tie to pull or restrain the other
But only to lead and assist.
Lord, bless the tie that binds these lives in Christian marriage.

Big Hands and Little Hands

For my Dad, with daily newfound understanding,
and constantly renewed respect.

I miss Big Hands
Big Hands came first
Holding, caring, and full of warmth
Big Hands helped and pointed and taught.
Hands that worked and carried, and
seemed strong enough for anything
Hands that could hold you tight, and keep you safe
Big Hands were always ready to hold Little Hands

Little Hands came later
Tiny hands at first
Amazing and intricate and perfect
Little Hands that reached to hold
So small and yet so full of love
Circling only one of your fingers as they took their first steps
But reaching out to hold the whole world

Little Hands watching Big Hands for lessons
and example, to point and to teach
Straining all the while to make their own grasp as bold
Asking for help, never doubting that
Big Hands could make or mend

We Laughed At Her Funeral

Big Hands could do anything

Big Hands have become smaller now
But their strength has not faded
The power of their love has grown stronger
My own hands still reach for theirs
The Little Hands grow bigger daily

and holding them tightly cannot keep them small
Those Little Hands are reaching now
for things beyond my grasp

How privileged a place it is, to stand in the middle
Reaching up for support from the Big Hands before me
Holding tightly to the Little Hands at my side
Bridging the gap between them
And being a better man for them both

J. Michael Grimes
Tennessee Mountain Solitude
August 24, 2003

A Day Too Late

A remembrance.

When should you do the things you should do?
When will be A Day Too Late?
When will you know the things you should know?
When should you ask the questions
that cannot wait another day?
For today was A Day Too Late.

Tell me that story just once again, I
want to remember the details.
Show me that skill, honed by years of
practice, so I'm sure it's never lost.
Teach me that lesson you learned so
well, so I can pass it along.
But today is A Day Too Late.

You put everything in its place, and it
was the best place for everything.
But I still can't find the things I need.
I would ask, and you would be so happy to share.
But today is A Day Too Late

You gave me everything I needed and so much more.
But I should have asked again.
Stories. Lessons. A distillation of an amazing life.
And I only scratched the surface.

We Laughed At Her Funeral

Memories. Experience. Reasons and truths
that only come through a long life lived.
Every word sincere and full of value.
How much more I could have had if only
I hadn't waited A Day Too Late.

You hid your generosity and worked
your Godly tasks in silence.
You gave of yourself without thought of reward.
You taught, and you touched, and all
for a glory beyond yourself.
You were a rock of faith, values, and honorable
presence to everyone who knew you.
Many admired you, though you shrugged such praise aside.
Many more would have been blessed by your wisdom,
if only they hadn't come A Day Too Late.

For myself, I could have had more, if I had only asked.
But I waited A Day Too Late.

What you gave was more than enough;
more than anyone could ask.
So I hold what you gifted to me and will treasure it forever.
All the lessons I needed to know.

And none of them could have come
A Day Too Soon.

J. Michael Grimes
Lakeland, Florida
April 2022

The Measure of A Man

How do you measure a man?
What makes him great or small?
Does it have to do with his appearance?
Does his stature count a lot?
His smile, his style, and the way he wears
His clothes, do they really make the man?

How much does charm count in the measuring,
Does it advance him to the front?
Does public acclaim and honors won,
A greater man create?

How does God measure a man?
What makes him great or small?
I think He judges by the heart,
And kindness counts a lot.
Words and deeds from thoughts begin,
Reflecting what the heart holds dear.

God knows the man whose heart is big,
Who is quick to help and slow to hurt.
No matter the number of good deeds done,
With God, the motive matters more.

How do you measure a man?

We Laughed At Her Funeral

What makes him great or small?
Only God can say for sure,
But I think He measures by the heart.

As Others See Me

I wonder if I would like me if I met me on the street.
Would my passing glance linger long enough to see,
Or would it quickly dart some other way?

Would my eyes meet mine directly,
Or pretend to focus somewhere else,
If I met me on the street?

Would I extend a friendly smile, a nod,
Or would I simply stay aloof,
If I met me on the street?

Would I see me as I really am,
Or would I scan for flaws to find,
If I met me on the street?

I wonder if I would like me,
I hope that I would like me,
I think that I would like me,
If I met me on the street.

To Our Grandparents

Little kittens and little kids,
A mess on the floor,
A garden of flowers, it is never a bore.
A workshop of tools, sewing with spools,
It is Our Grandparents' house.
Full of fun and no rules,
From Rattles and diapers,
To boyfriends galore,
You feel a warm feeling,
As you walk through the door.
We smile, laugh, and giggle some too.
We hope you know we will always love you.
Time has gone by so fast, too fast it seems,
However, the memories still make our hearts gleam!

From all of your girls,

Holly K. Grimes

Invocation for Missions

Our Father which art in heaven,
Our Father which art in our midst here and now,
Our Father which doth abide in every Christian heart,
We thank you for your presence.
You give so much—we acknowledge so little.
You answer our prayers—we ask for more.
You forgive us our mistakes—we repeat them.
You solve our problems—we create more.
Forgive us.

You have asked us to love one another and to serve one another.
You have asked us to reflect the life of Christ in our own daily lives.
You have commanded us to go into the world and share your love.
Make us willing.

Let this time of worship be a personal renewal of commitment in each of us.
We ask a special blessing on the obedient ones literally living the great commission,
And on each of us on our own personal mission field.
Thank you for those whose mission field today is the kitchen,
Those who prepared the food and the tables,
And those who will clean up after us.

We Laughed At Her Funeral

Bless this food and this day and make us aware of your perpetual blessings.
Amen

Life In Any Lane

Life is a lot like driving in Atlanta. You have to get in the correct lane and go with the flow. Don't look ahead, or it will scare you to death. Don't look back, because you can't go that direction anyway. Watch out for others, because they tend to butt in where they shouldn't. Know where you want to go and follow directions, or you might end up some place you don't want to be. Don't stop, no matter what. *"Pray without ceasing" (1 Thessalonians 5:17).*

When

I'm traveling every day, every minute,
Toward a very special place in time.
I've been on this quest for as long as I can remember.
I seem to think that everything
I want or need is there,
And everything I want to do will be done there.
Every answer to every problem will be there.
I am on my way to When.

". . .do not worry about tomorrow, for tomorrow will worry
about itself. Each day has enough trouble of its own"
(Matthew 6:34).

WHY

If I do what I do for the Lord, He will judge it.
He knows all I do, and my honest, innermost motive for doing it.

If the deed doesn't please Him, He will let me know.
If it does, it shouldn't offend or hurt anyone else.

I wonder why I try so hard to please people.
Why do I need human applause?

"Take heed that ye do not your alms before men, to be seen of them: otherwise ye have no reward of your Father which is in heaven" (Matthew 6:1).

Getting At the Truth

"You shouldn't say things like that. What will people think?"
"I don't care what people think."
"Sure you do. Everyone cares."
"Not me."
"I don't believe that."
"Why should I care?"
"Because what other people think about us makes us feel good or bad."
"Wrong! I decide how I feel."
"No wonder you are so unpopular."
"I'm not unpopular."
"Sure you are."
"Who says I am?"
"Everyone."
"Like who?"
"Why do you care?"
"I just do. That's all."
"I thought so."

Yesterday's Sandcastles

Walking on the beach recently, very early in the morning, I passed what was left of a large, detailed sandcastle. I continued walking and thinking. What I had seen there was the remains of someone's yesterday. I wondered about that person—who they were, what they were doing today, and if they had any thoughts today about how they had spent yesterday.

I too build many castles—not necessarily out of sand. I build castles in the air that never come to be. I start projects that never get finished. I write stories that never see pen and paper. While I throw together a quick meal, I plan the gourmet one I am going to prepare next. I rearrange my fabric stash and match it up repeatedly with different patterns before I put it all away again. I walk in the garden and talk to the flowers about how I am going to move them into or out of their present location for one reason or another, and I buy seeds and decide where to plant each variety, but they never escape the package. I decide which shrubs need pruning the next time I am outdoors. I open my mail and compose newsy replies to friends from over the years, but they never receive them. I think of shut-ins I know and nice things I could do for them one of these days—so many plans that never happen... so many castles, never built. So what am I doing instead? What do I have to show for all those yesterdays besides necessities and wasted time? I have regret and disappointment.

This is the day, with the Lord's help, I am going to start enjoying my life, not seeing how much I can cram into it. Most of what clutters my mind, and keeps me awake at night, and my stomach churning, and my jaws clenched, and my eyes full of ready tears is excess. I allow things and people to control me, drive me, and cause me to miss the things that count. I will start now, cleaning out and sharing with others. I will not force myself to do anything unnecessary. I will be kind, helpful, and available, but I will not feel responsible for everyone, or take on the job of fixing others. I will cherish my husband and children and my friends. I will stop collecting. Just because I like it, I do not need to have it. I will be more frugal with everything–time, money, food, and I will give as much as I can. I really love giving.

I will do things for people, not because I should, but because I want to, and make things for the fun of it and not just for last-minute gifts. I will do one project at a time and experience the pleasure that comes from finishing, I will read more; I will write more. I will begin cleaning out the garage of my life as well as the one I have to fight my way through every time I leave the house. I will dispose of the things that steal away my time and my peace of mind. I will enjoy all the seasoning God has sprinkled life with, like nature, music, and children. I will savor the aroma of a new bar of soap, the smell of a lumberyard, which brings memories of my dad. I will lie in the grass and find angels in the clouds. I will take time to taste the food I eat and feel the warm sun on my back. I will not be too busy to do the kind things my heart desires to do; I will bake homemade bread to share and not count the calories. I will do the things I need to do, but this year I will leave a trail of real sandcastles everywhere I go.

Life is a gift from God. Every gift is different, everyone a unique design, and everyone with a divine purpose. Life is precious and not a moment should slip away unaware.

> So here hath been dawning another blue day;
> Think, wilt thou let it slip useless away?
> Out of eternity this new day is born;
> Into eternity at night will return. *T. Carlyle*

"This is the day the Lord hath made; we will rejoice and be glad in it" (Psalm 118:24).

Prayer Without Words

To say that I am at a loss for words would probably raise eyebrows or prompt a questioning glance among those who know me. Hard as it might be to believe, I sometimes run out of words. However, I never ever run out of thoughts. There are times when I wish I could put my mind on pause. It leaps from here to there, from now to yesterday, or ahead to things yet to come. It flashes from good thoughts to frightening ones as quickly as lightning and loses track of time and other important things. It is difficult to reign my mental rambling into the moment, and almost impossible to keep it captive. This sporadic behavior of my mental control results in all kinds of distractions, forgetfulness, confusion, and lost items of all kinds–even things as large as my car in the parking lot.

With the acceptance that I am not likely to change, I can usually recover well enough as to not be too obvious, by making a wisecrack, or by switching topics halfway through my out-of-control overgrowth of thought. However, on a more serious note, this avalanche of thoughts does handicap my prayer life. I often think of something to bring before the Lord and before I can find the right way to phrase the words, my thoughts have been crowded out by others. I start to pray about one thing which reminds me to pray about another…and that about another, and so it goes. There are other times, usually when I need most to pray,

Prayer Without Words

that no words will come at all. Sometimes the words I need are not among the words I have stored. Have you ever desperately needed to feel God's presence and to pour out your heart, but could not? Have you ever asked a son or daughter, a friend, or a pastor to pray for you because you could not phrase your needs? Have you ever felt as if you were just mouthing familiar words, scriptures, or someone else's prayers?

There are times when I have to remind myself that talking to God does not require form or words. I know that when one prays in public it is necessary to think in a logical order so that those hearing and praying along can easily follow. However, a personal, sincere prayer does not need to be expressed in complete sentences or poetic phrases. God hears thoughts.

My son took a college class in speed reading and devoured it. Today he can read a page faster than I can turn one. I was skeptical, of course, how he could both comprehend and still enjoy reading that way. I doubted that he could savor the sound and feel of the words and phrases. In his condensed explanation, he told me that he no longer read word-by-word but that he looked at blocks of words. His primary example to me was that you can pick up piles of laundry from the floor much faster than you can pick up one sock at a time, and still not miss anything. He referred to reading blocks of thought rather than words. The thoughts then created mental pictures, which were easily stored in his memory.

I decided to experiment with praying in thoughts,

rather than in specific words. I stopped composing and started thinking. Sitting in my comfortable, familiar chair early in the morning and watching the sun slowly move closer from the end of the curving street, smelling the aroma of coffee from the warm mug in my hands, and hearing the birds exchanging signals in the trees outside the window, I thought about what a magnificent God we have. When my mind wandered to yesterday's mistakes, I confessed my shortcomings and thought about the gift of a new day to do better. When my mind shifted to my family and friends, I thought how thankful I was for answered prayers. When I looked at my list of those in need of prayers, I thought about each one and asked for God's blessing.

It is working for me; thought by thought, I pray. One by one, just as they flit in and out of my mind, I share them with God. Any place I am, any need I see, any emotion I experience, thought prayers are as close to God as I can get. He needs no instructions from me: no details, no specifics, no PowerPoint presentations or visual aids. All during the day, I just pray without words.

I often recall words or thoughts I have read or heard that had meaning for me, but I forget where they originated. So it is with this acronym for prayer entitled, *Prayer results in ACTS*. When my thoughts are hopelessly jumbled, it helps me to cover the basics:

A stands for Adoration,
C stands for Confession,
T stands for Thanksgiving,

S stands for Supplication and Submission.

"Pray without ceasing" (1 Thessalonians 5:17).

Are You Listening???

"My husband says I don't listen. At least I think that is what he said."

That cute little plaque hanging in my friend's hallway caught my attention and made me smile. "Guilty as charged." I confessed to myself.

"Listening to another drummer, were you?" Thoreau might have asked.

"Yes," I would have to answer, and very possibly, it would be to my own drumming. It could very well be my own thoughts I'm concentrating on, or the response I am composing in my mind. It could be a more interesting conversation nearby, or a mental list I am compiling for later. It could even be boredom, because unfortunately I am not always interested in what the speaker is telling me. I might just be in a hurry.

Good listeners are not hard to recognize. They look at me while they listen and not over my shoulder, and they do not interrupt my chain of thought with topics of their own. They ask questions to be sure they understand. I know they hear me because their responses match my comments. Real listeners appear more interested in what I am saying than in telling me what they are thinking, or in their own rebuttal. The truth be known, I probably talk more to them than I intend because they make me feel like what I am saying is something they want to hear. Good

Are You Listening???

listeners are unselfish. It requires their time, concentration, patience, and sometimes their self-control. They listen to understand rather than to oppose.

It is not hard to spot those who are not listening either. One clue is that you can stop in the middle of a sentence, and they don't even notice. Their unrelated replies sometimes give them away. Interruptions signal their impatience to tell you something they think is more important than what you are telling them. If they doodle, tap or shuffle papers it appears they are anxious to end the conversation.

Hearing and listening—what is the difference? Hearing involves sound entering your ears, listening goes farther and sticks to something inside your head, your heart, or even your memory. Any teacher will tell you that learning is as dependent on listening as digestion is on chewing and swallowing. Sympathy and empathy are a result of listening and so are our memories. Listening is vital to true friendship. How else can we get to really know and understand another?

Listening is not all giving. The experiences of others are an endless source of information for the listener, and sometimes provide insights into human nature. While we are not to judge others, listening to them sometimes explains their attitudes and behaviors. If you are a good enough listener, you might even hear things they do not know they are telling you. Ima Bragger likes to talk about her achievements and her importance, when what she really wants you to know is, "Your admiration will sustain me."

We Laughed At Her Funeral

The self-centered conversations, actions, and mannerisms of the Town Crier could be shouting "Look at me, listen to me, I am important too." Could Teddy Bear, who tells each of us what we want to hear and changes viewpoints constantly to please everyone really be asking, "If I don't cross you, will you love me?" Translated, it may be that Notso Pious' detailed reporting on the problems of others and the public tell-all prayer requests could be another way of saying, "Have you heard the latest?" Then there is Accuse You who projects his own character flaws onto others, which in turn makes him suspicious of the rest of us. It makes him feel better to say, "I know what you are up to!" We cannot forget Whiney Poo, who likes best to talk only of aches, pains, and misfortune. Her cry is, "I am more pitiful than you." If we are listening, we know these are needy people.

Probably the biggest problem that I have with listening is that I cannot both talk and listen at the same time, and my default appears to be set on talking. When my mouth opens, my ears close. Maybe that is why Hamlet said, "Give every man thine ear, but few thy voice," and some unknown author, the cliche "God gave us two ears and one mouth so that we could listen twice as much as we talk."

Scripture plainly tells us that God has given us different gifts, and I have no doubt that the art of listening is one of them. Gifted or not, it is a skill that we can all learn with practice, and what better place to start than with people who long to be heard. We are all needy in God's sight, and we know that He listens with His full attention to each of us. He also speaks. Are we listening?

> *"While he was still speaking, a cloud enveloped them, and a voice from the cloud said, "This is my Son, whom I love; with him I am well pleased. Listen to him!" (Matthew 17:5).*

When I Grow Up

God has been good to me in too many ways to even begin to name, but the blessing of grandchildren is at the top of my list. There is nothing to compare with babies, and I am sure there is magic involved in the way they latch on to my heart at birth. Just when it seems that they can't get any sweeter or cuter, they turn into toddlers and entwine my heart. From then on there is no escape. Every age seems to be the best, even though the attention they require sometimes separates me from my rocking chair, and heart-hurting situations invariably occur from time to time.

Then one day when I least expect it, they are no longer children, and I have to step back and turn loose. They want to grow up, I want to keep them little. The love between us remains, but the stage changes, and the script changes and so does the setting. They go to college, or get married, or go to work and our time apart grows longer and longer. Their world is full of new and different adventures, while mine is comfortable in the way things have always been. Even communicating with them is difficult sometimes. I have felt this metamorphosis even more with our grandchildren than with their parents.

I have been turning all this over in my mind recently because two more of the grandchildren finished their graduate programs this month. Another is planning a wedding, and others are adding great grandchildren to our numbers. With all of that in mind, consider my reaction to the following article written and shared with me by one of them.

"One thing I often wish I had understood as a child was that grownups are not invincible. Fortunately for me, I grew up blissfully naïve to the words stress and worry. I knew nothing of their definitions, let alone that my parents might experience them. To me, my parents were always happy. The rare times when they got angry or looked sad could be explained by my brothers' misbehavior, or Dad forgetting the milk. Knowing better now, I consider myself blessed that I grew up in a happy home, with both sets of grandparents as well as every aunt, uncle, cousin, and relative living within 30 minutes away.

The words 'grown up' are a sort of conundrum. To be grown implies that you have finished growing; that you have reached the final level and there can be no more growth. But do we ever really stop growing? It is easy to see the growth between your toddler years, pre-adolescence, and becoming a hormone-enhanced teenager. It is not until college and the years after that we really start thinking that we must grow-up and get our first real job, first apartment, learn to live on a budget, etc. This in turn, for the lucky ones, leads to marriage and a family. 1 have heard that the second child is much easier because we have learned all the tricks the first time around. We grow, and we grow, and we grow.

So, when are we considered a grown up? What criterion

is necessary to be grown? Do you have to own a house? Have a family? Do your children have to be grown? Or is it simply a maturity level? The older we get the wiser we are perceived. One thing some of us are the most ignorant about is that our parents and grandparents are still growing and maturing themselves. They still face new challenges and dilemmas. They might be different from ours, but they still have to face them. Just as I struggle and fail, so do they, no matter the age. It is difficult to see past our own circumstances and put ourselves in others' shoes. It is impossible to know how others feel, or to understand why they react the way they do.

My grandparents are the wisest people I know. They have been through so many experiences and have survived many challenges. They have raised three children and have helped raise my siblings and me. I am constantly talking to my grandmother about my problems. She prays for many things. Sometimes for a specific need, sometimes for guidance, sometimes just to mention to God that I need an extra angel looking after me. She often says (paraphrased) 'I wish I had an answer for you. Let's pray for guidance and trust that God will help you through this.' I believe that my experiences also help her to grow as well. My grandmother (at the time of this writing) is 78 years old. If she is still growing, who in the world is fully grown?

I am 24 years old, and all I want to be is a grownup. I want people to look at me and see a mature young adult and not a little girl. Yet, I sense that the idea of being grown is just an illusion. Maybe the point is that we will never stop growing. God is the only true grownup. He is the only person that has experienced everything. He sees all, hears all, and knows all."

Anna Carol Porter
May 2014

"So the one who plants is not important and the one who waters is not important. Only God is important, because He is the one who makes things grow"
(I Corinthians 3:7).

Where Have the Heroes Gone?

Do you recall the picture books written and illustrated for children by the artist Martin Handford, entitled, *Where's Waldo?* The pages were filled margin to margin with a maze of brightly colored pictures painted into a dense collage that was hiding the little hero, Waldo. The object was to find Waldo somewhere among all the other people, pets, and objects on the page. The pictures always included a few larger, brighter, and obvious distractions and a scattering of very small items to make Waldo harder to find. I thought the books were wonderful for several reasons, but mainly because they kept the children occupied for long periods of time.

It has been a long time since I opened the pages of one of those books, but occasionally I open my eyes to what is going on around me in the world and I feel as if I am living right smack in the middle of one of those books. Waldo is not the only thing lost in all the surrounding distractions. Neither is he the only lost soul.

It seems that much of the life I am accustomed to is being painted over with change. Progress has been well received for obvious reasons: I like the electronics that make my life easier. I enjoy the exciting new discoveries and opportunities that have made life easier and more fun.

Where Have the Heroes Gone?

I am thankful for the miraculous medical advances that benefit us all. What seems more and more difficult to find in the maze are the small, personal, human interactions. It seems as if the good things that still abound among us are in the shadows of larger, more sensational ones. The ordinary people that make the world keep running are hidden behind those more powerful. The natural and the beautiful things we value are being covered over with things ugly and vulgar.

I know the good is still there, but it is harder and harder for me to find. Maybe I am just not looking hard enough or in the right places. Take heroes for instance. I know the world is still full of everyday heroes, but because my observation of the world outside my own small domain is largely based on what I see on the nightly news, the internet, and the television, I don't see them. They are small and hidden behind the glaring headlines of crime, politics, and sports, or the glamour of celebrities and entertainment.

When I was a kid, I thought of a hero as someone who could fly faster than a speeding bullet. As a teenager my hero was handsome and rode a Palomino horse named Trigger. The words "hero" and "love" are alike in that they are sometimes very loosely defined.

Since then, I have known some real heroes. My brother was a hero to those he air-lifted off the battlegrounds in Vietnam. Just yesterday I read about a young man who gave his life diving into a lake and rescuing a small child. While a few of the most outstanding are still recognized, the everyday heroes are just people among us who make an important difference for good in the life of another.

When I considered that broader definition of a hero, I realized that I have been covered my whole life by one hero after another. Everyone reading this probably knows someone personally who is a hero or heroine. You, very likely, are a hero yourself to someone.

I found some other interesting definitions while researching the word hero. For example, Roswell Hitchcock described a hero as "...one who was always doing or dying for another." I chuckled at William Rotsler's definition as "...one who thinks slower than a coward."

Becoming a hero is not something we do for ourselves or for recognition or for fame or for reward. It happens when we do what needs to be done for the good of another. I believe we can all be a hero to someone. Why not start by leading an unbeliever to Christ, and thus save their life for eternity?

> *Our Heavenly Father, thank you for the heroes among us who are obeying your command to love others as themselves and to love You with all their hearts. Amen*

Part Five

Letters Shared

Sometimes I want to say something meaningful to someone, but the words take too long to come to me and what I say doesn't express exactly what I am thinking. However, I've found that with a pen, paper, and a few minutes of quiet time I'm able to convey my message more precisely. It also gives me opportunity to rethink my words.

A Letter... Finally Written

No one that knows me very well will be surprised to hear me say, "I'm a little late writing this letter." It should've been written years and years ago when I knew for sure the recipient would receive it. Now, I can only hope.

Dear Miss Anna:

I was only one of many, many that you taught Bible stories to after school once a week in the basement of our small town library. I'm sure you don't remember my name or my rosy, red face. There was never anything to set me apart from all the others during those years, unless, of course, you remember my singing voice. Back then I still sang out loudly, with all my heart, the Bible songs you played on the old upright piano, and with no idea I was off key or that I was a monotone. I'm glad you didn't tell me.

Even so, I remember you. I didn't understand then why grownups called you the "old-maid missionary." You weren't old at all, and I thought you were beautiful. In my mind missionaries were plain and drab, lived in far off lands, and taught natives about Jesus. You definitely didn't meet that description. I now know that you truly were a for-real missionary, and I was one of the needy natives. Even though I can no longer bring your face to my mind's eye, I do remember that your voice was soft, your smile was warm, and you loved us all.

You called the after-school gathering, Bible School, and that's just what it was. The Bible stories I learned from you are as vivid today as they were all those years ago. It was from your flannel storyboard I first saw the Bible come to life. It's where I watched Paul, the harsh, mean Roman who was then named Saul, fall down in the bright, blinding light from heaven on the road to Damascus and heard Jesus speak to him *(Acts, Chapter 9)*. It was also there I saw Daniel put into a den with lions, but because he trusted God and had been obedient, I saw the lions shut their mouths and not harm him *(Daniel, Chapter 6)*.

I loved the story of the little boy Samuel who heard God call his name in the night three times, and how Eli told him not to be frightened but to listen to what God wanted to tell him *(Samuel, Chapter 3)*. I can still see Joseph's many-colored coat and remember how his jealous brothers sold him as a slave, then told their father he had been killed. Even after doing that, Joseph forgave them and saved them from famine *(Genesis, Chapter 37)*. There were many more adventure stories and other heroes, and the images still march across the flannel board of my mind.

Your story of Ipsey and Newman has stayed with me all my life. You told us we all have both good and bad in our hearts and they constantly fight. Ipsey was born in our hearts and is our bad nature. He tries to make us think and do wrong things. When we ask Jesus into our hearts, Newman moves in and he tells us what is right and good. When we listen to Ipsey and do what is wrong, he

A Letter... Finally Written

wins the battle. When we listen to Newman and choose to do what is right, Newman wins. You told us we always choose the winner and thereby the ruler of our heart, and the flannel storyboard showed either a big Ipsey or a big Newman sitting on the throne in our heart. I learned from you that it's okay to ask God when I need something, and I should always remember to thank Him. You taught us being nice to other people is the same as being nice to God, and whenever we hurt someone else by word or deed, we hurt God too.

How I wish I could sit down again in that dimly lighted basement with the dusty, damp smell and the big round pillars holding up the ceiling and listen again while you tell a story with the magical flannel storyboard. Of course, the storyboard has long sense been replaced with a television or a computer screen. Who knows how many hours you must have spent creating the colorful Bible characters backed with flannel that brought the stories to life? More importantly, only God knows just how far the ripple that began in your afternoon Bible School has spread.

You told us once that when we get to heaven everyone else who's there because of our influence would be standing beside us. Whether or not you ever read this letter, I hope you know I'll be standing beside you in Heaven.

From a little girl grown up.

Sadness

Dear Friend:

I have been where you are now, and I remember how it felt. Friends and loved ones aware of my grieving kept telling me I should close the door on sadness and go on. For me it was better to leave the door ajar and allow my emotions to circulate. Sometimes the hurt came roaring through like a strong wind and whipped me unexpectedly. Other times it settled around me like a cold, chilling draft I could not escape. All the while, like the wind, the sadness kept moving on. After a while the bad began to dissipate, and I could see the good. Now I can slip in and out of that door to the past at my pleasure, without the grief.

> *"And the God of all grace, who called you to his eternal glory in Christ, after you have suffered a little while, will himself restore you and make you strong, firm and steadfast" (1 Peter 5:10).*

About That Question

Dear Big Brother:

We have some interesting conversations on the phone, don't we? The only problem is when we get serious we both get emotional. When we communicate on the internet though, we can't interrupt one another. That's a good thing. Another good thing is I can read and reread what I have said before I send it. That way I can be sure I have said what I meant to say and be prepared to debate, because you *will* want to debate.

I've been thinking about something we talked about the other night. You said you weren't worried about dying, but didn't know what to expect after that. I guess none of us knows what to expect, but scripture says that what God has planned for us is like nothing we've ever seen or heard or even imagined. So, how could we know? Considering what I've seen of His handiwork so far, that sounds good enough for me. I trust many things I don't understand. I don't know how an elevator works, or how electricity does what it does, or what keeps great heavy planes in the air, but I'm not going to stop using them just because I don't understand how they work. I think that is called faith.

Maybe what it will be like isn't what bothers you. Maybe it's your passport. You used to be a good Bible scholar. Remember how we argued about our different church doctrines? I thought yours was much too strict and was based on fear, while you thought mine was all watered down. I still think I was right. Remember the Pharisees and all their do's and don'ts? They had so many rules and regulations that no one could live by them in the first place, or enjoy life if they could. Ask me if I think we still have modern-day Pharisees who like to complicate Christianity and scare people away.

Christ made it simple. It's our hearts that He's interested in, and when our hearts are right it just follows that we'll love Him and others. When we love Him and others, the other commandments are natural outcomes and common sense rules that make our lives better. Think about it. He warned us about certain things because of the consequences. It is no different than when we tell our kids what to avoid so they won't get hurt or hurt others. Like our kids, sometimes we follow His advice, but a lot of the time we don't. I'm sure He watches us mess up daily just like we see our kids making wrong decisions. He wishes we would just listen for our own good, but He doesn't love us any less. I think His heart goes out to those of us who need help the most. God isn't a dictator who wants to take all the pleasure out of life, but a heavenly parent who wants only good things for us. The rules are necessary for us to be happy and healthy and helpful.

Then we come to your question, "What about me, though? I've really messed up. I've broken most of the rules and made nearly all of the mistakes. I've probably used up all of my grace."

About That Question

Not so. Think about these guys. King David was special to God from the time he was a little boy. God protected him from all kinds of things, including a giant, but David committed the big sin, Bathsheba! That wasn't bad enough; he even had her husband murdered. When David confessed his sin, God said, "Okay, David. Let's start over and do better this time." God saw David's repenting heart. Then there was Noah. He must have had a lot going for him to have been chosen as the contractor for the Ark. Yet the first thing he did when he got on dry land was to get sloppy drunk and sleep with his daughter-in-law. God saw genuine remorse in his heart though, and gave him a fresh start too. Remember Paul? He went hunting for Christians to kill and later became the greatest preacher of all time.

I believe, and this is important, the basis of my personal faith is that God sees my heart. I could never live by all the man-made rules. God wishes I wouldn't mess up for my own sake and the sake of others, but He doesn't stop loving me when I do. Remember, too, that God is our judge, not others. What's in the heart tells the real story, and we can't fool Him. We either love God and others or we don't, and our actions give us away. All the other do's and don'ts, should's and should nots, are covered by the command to love God and love one another.

Sometimes you jokingly call me a saint... far from it. Like everyone I have a lot of hang-ups, but I do live from the heart and I do love a lot and maybe that's what you see. I know you better than you know yourself and despite your tough act, I know for a fact you have a good, tender heart. While living the Christian life includes going to church, tithing, and serving, it's also about tolerance, patience, kindness, and forgiveness—things that naturally come from a good heart. It isn't the hard task some would have us believe. When I think of Christ, as I see him in the scriptures, He was never hard on people, but dealt with them with a kind and gentle spirit. He didn't scare sinners off, He won them over.

That's enough of this. Just remember how you and I love one another, and that God loves us so much more. Now that is a lot! Accept the fact and stop torturing yourself with doubt and worry. God's grace is sufficient. Talk it over with Him. He says things so much better.

Love,
Sis

Two Roads To the Same Place

Dear Friend:

Our first encounter was at a Mother-Daughter Banquet where you were the guest speaker. Without my knowledge, the seating had been pre-arranged by a mutual friend who thought the two of us should become acquainted. As difficult as it is to believe, knowing we're both so introverted, we wasted not a moment engaging in a conversation that has never waned. I was repeatedly amazed at how many times you spoke my thoughts and expressed my exact ideas almost in the same words I was thinking. It was immediately obvious to me that we shared many of the same ideals, values, and ambitions.

When you began your presentation, you used the dollhouse from your youth as a prop, while you told stories about your growing up years, room by room. As you talked, I recalled the corresponding years of my life. Again, I was astounded. There was no way our childhoods could have been more different. Your life was as far removed from mine as possible, and yet here we were. We were so alike, but the products of very different environments.

Your friendship has influenced me, comforted me, entertained, and inspired me. You have listened, as you do so well, and you have encouraged me to write and increased my confidence in that area. I must admit, you have been a very challenging competitor in my quest to be the center of attention at certain gatherings.

Aside from all of the above, my friend, I will be eternity grateful to you for the self-sacrifice you have shown in your faithful dedication to living out my fantasies of becoming a published author, a much-loved public speaker, and especially for frequently enjoying the culture and countryside of England in my place.

Thank you, my friend. We have traveled different roads and that has made–almost no difference.

Fondly,

a Kindred Spirit

Thank You Note

Dear friend:

Thank you for the time we've had to spend with one another, and for the confidences and hopes and troubles that we've shared. Thank you for the understanding we've brought to one another, for the patience we've had with each other's faults, and for the advice and even scoldings we were able to give each other without anyone taking offense.

Thank you for the help we've been to each other in so many ways. Because of you, I'm a better, happier person, and maybe you have grown too, because of me. Thank you for the assurance that you would give me anything in your power: time, money, possession, encouragement, or sympathy, whatever my need, and that you know I would be as quick to respond. Thank you that we could laugh together, cry together, and rejoice together.

Adapted from a very old framed poem.
Author Unknown

Keep Your Heart

Dear Granddaughter:

You came into our world on a strong winter wind and brought with you a blizzard that made history. It was Christmas time, and what a wonderful gift you were. Because you spent so many weekends with us during your early years, we had the privilege and the pleasure of being a close part of your life as you grew up and the memories fill our hearts to overflowing.

Our pictures tell the story of getting so dirty in Grandmother's garden, fun with cousins, playing in Granddaddy's swing, and a trip to the Little River.

How many Easter dresses were made especially for you and how many Halloween costumes? Too many to count! Our Christmas parties, with all the family on Christmas Eve, have never changed even though each of us have.

Now that you are grown up, our times together are fewer but our love for one another is no less. We still squeeze in time to alter a prom dress, to meet a new beau, or to celebrate a special occasion. Phone calls are only a thought away.

You are an exceptionally pretty young lady. My mother always said it was nice to be pretty, but to remember that no matter what one did to the outside, what's on the inside would always show through. So nourish your soul and spirit, as well as your body, and continue to be kind and loving and good. That will keep you beautiful.

Granddaddy and I cherish you in our hearts. We thank our wonderful heavenly Father for giving you to us and for taking care of you through the years. We pray that you will always trust Him with your life.

GM & GD

Heart of a Shepherd

Dear Pastor:

It seems as though I begin every note or letter I write the same way, with an apology for not having written sooner. This one is no exception. However timely or not, it's sincere.

In the thirty-plus years I belonged to the same church, you were the pastor who best met my needs. I have known it for a long time and I have talked about it with others who share my feelings, but I have never told you. Since I like to be told when I have done something right, I thought you might also.

Your sermons were uncomplicated, yet profound, and always left me with something to carry around in my mind the following week. Your positive messages made doing the right thing sound so good that I was anxious to get to it. Rather than scolding me for the wrongs I had already done or surely would, you never let me forget that God still loved me.

When I think about you, the same two things always come to my mind, humility and sincerity. You spoke to us from the pulpit as if you yourself were at the same time part of the congregation, struggling with all the same things we were. You had a way of lifting us up rather than beating us down. Most of all I have come to appreciate your honesty, even the measure of dishonesty which seems to unavoidably creep into the business of running a church.

I understand why God likened us to sheep. We are so easily lost, frightened, and confused. If we, His sheep, are His most precious creation, He must select his shepherds carefully and what an honor to be chosen. Forgive us when we busy ourselves measuring you with unreliable gauges of our own making, forgetting that service for God can only be measured by Him. Since He has promised to reward each of us accordingly, what is man's favor in comparison?

By now you are wondering what the point is for this letter, and I'm not sure. Whatever it may be, it's also a thank you for your contribution to my spiritual growth. I don't know anything at all about your present situation, but I hope all is well with you, your very special family, and your congregation. I pray that God will continue to use you in the very special way that is you.

A Hard Choice

Dear Little One:

Of course you are scared. It's a little like getting a divorce yourself. You were together with all those you love and now you are apart from them. All divorces aren't as painful as the one in your family. Some people divorce when they realize they each want something different from life, but remain friends and continue to care for one another. When that doesn't happen it forces all the other members of the family to make hard decisions also. You are supposed to love them both. I would be very disappointed if you didn't.

This isn't about you, even though it affects you. This isn't a competition, but a decision. Whatever your choice, someone will feel you have turned away from them. To complicate things even more, each one involved is viewing the same situation from their own perspective. Can you possibly make everyone happy? You already know the answer to that. While I don't want you to disregard the feelings of others, you do have to choose what is best for you, just as everyone else involved has to do for themselves. It doesn't mean you are choosing one over another, but that you are choosing yourself.

So many things I want to say, but I'm sure by now you have had so much advice that it is bouncing off your

A Hard Choice

head. Anyway, you can only move ahead one day at a time, and if you worry you might worry about the wrong thing and waste all that perfectly good worry. It is not good to be wasteful.

Memorize my favorite Bible verse for times like this and believe it. It will make you feel so much better. Never underestimate your own worth. I am always here for you.

> *"Do not be anxious about anything, but in everything, by prayer and petition, with thanksgiving, present your requests to God. And the peace of God, which transcends all understanding, will guard your heart and your mind in Christ Jesus" (Philippians 4:6).*

My Bad!

To A Former Co-worker:

You are often on my mind. Your life has affected mine in ways impossible to explain. God used your life to teach me many things I needed to know, and I want to thank you for those lessons learned.

My short-term exposure to your life made some long-term changes in mine. The difficulties you experienced on the job (some of which I contributed to), your troubled marriage (so carefully concealed), and your long illness are proof indeed that God can take every hurt and use it to help another. Through you, God taught me a lot about acceptance, tolerance, and especially about being judgmental. How seldom we really know the facts, and how impossible it is to make judgments without them. I saw, at your expense the hurt and misunderstanding that resulted. It's no wonder Christ told us not to judge others.

I am sorry that I, like the apostles long ago, didn't stand up for you when I should have. I pray that you, like Christ, will forgive me. I know now that God was preparing you for that important position you were designed for and have so successfully accomplished. I know you are now being commended by the very people who were your faultfinders, and I know one of the reasons God can use you to help others is because you have been there.

Thank you for the example that you set for me and for many others.

It Is Enough

Honey:

Ours is a good life. Look through the windows at the flowers, birds, squirrels, and trusting rabbits. See the noisy, curious grandchildren walking on the flowers, chasing after the beggarly squirrels, and frightening the bunny with an outstretched carrot. The first wild bunny they have ever seen and the first carrot that the bunny has ever seen.

It is the best life. Watch the trusting children chase the scampering squirrels while the tolerant kitty watches from under a chair. The grass is green, the sky is blue, and the breeze is making the shade dance under the trees.

I love our life. Blue jays, "red jays," and blackbirds share the bounty. Me, too! It is better than any video, because it is ours; yours and mine. It is a good life, isn't it?

It is enough.

THE REAL CHRISTMAS

I have loved Christmas through all the stages of my life. When I was young, it was all about gifts and goodies and a stocking filled with oranges and nuts. Sometime between those years and now, I came to understand that Christmas wasn't about the gifts we give and receive from one another at all, but about God's Gift to us and about us sharing Him with others.

In Search of Christmas Lost

In those semi-awake moments that come before a decent time to get up in the morning, I find I can think so clearly. Words fit together perfectly, and I submit reams of inspiration into the darkness. I did that just today, and during those intense moments of divine creativity I penned a masterpiece. However, like a morning mist, the message lingered briefly and then was gone.

I had been thinking about Christmas and remembering the joy it always brings. I doubt anyone has loved the season more. So when had that wonderful anticipation and excitement turned into a joyless list of things to be done?

In search of an answer, I took an Ebenezer Scrooge excursion. The first thing that came to mind was a Christmas Pageant I organized once with the other little kids in the neighborhood. We were so good that we took our show on the road or, should I say, on the street. I was the star because I was the only one who could read at the time; the others had to be mimes. The apex was being asked to perform at the church.

We were poor then, but that was okay because so was everyone else. Even though our gifts were few, we always got something we wanted. Mother made wonderful fluffy white divinity that melted in your mouth, and sometimes we had hard ribbon candy that was prettier to look at than it was good to eat. Even though I couldn't even sing Jingle Bells on key, I was allowed to bundle up and join the carolers and share the hot chocolate from grateful neighbors. December's issue of *Good Housekeeping* always pictured unique gingerbread houses to make, and while ours never looked like the pictures, we still had fun.

We could hardly wait for the first day of December when the downtown Christmas lights were turned on and for the stores to be decorated, knowing soon the first lighted tree would appear in someone's window. One year the church had a live nativity scene on the lawn and just standing there in the dark made me feel as if I were in Bethlehem. Putting up the Christmas tree was what I liked best, even though our decorations were skimpy and the tree lights only lasted until one bulb went out. It was then I promised myself that someday I would have a big tree with lots of lights.

Someday is here, and I have that big tree with lots and lots of lights and so much more. Now holiday decorations and ornaments, more plentiful and grand than ever, adorn the streets and stores even before the witches and goblins have had their day. There is no shortage of Santa Clauses to hold tots on their knees, even though his job has been greatly simplified with computerized lists and his role reduced to that of a photo salesman. Christmas music still fills the air, but most often from loud department store speakers and seldom from carolers. Occasionally even a familiar song is heard.

Competing with books and magazines full of Christmas ideas available all during the year, in store windows angels spread their wings over glittering gift boxes while wise men buy gifts of cologne, gold jewelry, and spirits. Exquisite crèches are for sale from even merchants whose faith denies the birth it portrays. Holiday food and entertainment defy description.

Now back to the question. When did anxiety and weariness replace the joy? I think it happened when I wandered too far from the simple, holy, uncluttered celebration of the shepherds and got caught up in the lavish extravagance of today's wise men. If I can but glean the best from all the years and relinquish the excess, I think I can, like Ebenezer, wake up to a happy and satisfying Christmas. How to do that? I don't know, but whatever my plan was, it sounded good when I was half asleep.

No Room In the Inn

It was the night before Christmas in Bethlehem town, and, "No room in the inn!" rang in their ears. The small town was crowded with travelers who'd come to be counted for the census. Tired and rowdy, the travelers shoved and pushed and searched in vain for a place to sleep.

Among the crowd, Mary and Joseph prayed they might find room in an inn. God's answer to them was more than they asked and better by far. The innkeeper could see that Mary's time had come and knew that the bustling, noisy, and uncomfortable inn wasn't the right place. He offered the stable, quiet and private, without even knowing that the baby to be born there was the Child of God.

Did Mary and Joseph stand out in the crowd, or did they blend in with others whose needs were the same? Did God set them apart and lighten their load, or were they like us with the same needs and concerns? Were they fearful and anxious as we would have been, or did their secret keep them calm and unafraid? Would the shepherds who were following the star that night have been welcome at the inn or turned quickly away? Would their response have been the same had they found Baby Jesus amid splendor, rather than cozy and content in swaddling clothes? Would the star have shined as brightly in the center of town as it did that night in the dark countryside?

From our present perspective, we know the answers to those questions because like an oil painting, the image is sharpest from a distance. We know the Christmas story beginning to end and all in between. From our vantage point, we can see God's hand in all that is past, yet we still struggle with day-to-day doubts. Despite all of God's promises in His great history book, we worry and fret and struggle with questions as if we had no help. That night in Bethlehem, in a divinely orchestrated plan, God gave us the answer to all of our questions. God, in the form of a tiny baby, stepped down to live among us here on earth and still today stands always at the door of our hearts. Let us never say, "No room in my inn."

> *"Behold, I stand at he door, and knock: if any man hear my voice, and open the door, I will come in to him, and will sup with him, and he with me" (Revelation 3:20).*

Christmas Light

"So live like children who belong to the light. Light brings every kind of goodness, right living, and truth" (Ephesians 5:8-9).

I love the beautiful Christmas trees in department stores that seem each year to be more original and elaborate. The themes change, the colors vary, and the beautifully crafted ornaments displayed on the branches tempt me to do something different with my tree each year, but I never do. What I really love is my real tree with special ornaments collected over the years, each with a memory engraved in my heart. And I love the lights. For me, the lights transform the tree into a living thing and reflect His presence. The lights brighten my spirits and they help keep away the shadows.

Shadows at Christmas? There shouldn't be, of course, but there's more to getting into the spirit of the holidays than putting up decorations and turning on the lights. Shadows can mean adding a lot more to an already full schedule and having too few resources to make the season bright. For many, shadows mean no tree, no gifts, no feasts of goodies, no one special to celebrate with, and no joy. Christmas as portrayed on lovely homespun greeting cards are fairy tales for those to whom the holiday has become a chore. Loneliness casts dark shadows on those separated from loved ones, and gift giving can turn a budget into a financial nightmare. Extra cooking, shopping, wrapping, visiting, and the scheduling in of special activities leaves little time for the peace and calm portrayed by the iconic images of the first Christmas. Excessive cheer and spirits frequently blot out all merriment. We have moved a long way away from the first Christmas in a borrowed stable.

Is it possible that there were shadows cast even on that first Christmas? Mary had a secret, as joyous as it was, she couldn't explain to the curious, judgmental, or unkind. Maybe there was hurtful gossip circulating in the small town where she was well known. Tears may have filled the eyes of Mary's mother when she overheard whispering about her child. The trip to Bethlehem must have been long and frightening for a young girl about to have her first baby a long way from home. Surely Joseph was concerned about finding room in an inn for Mary.

Yes, I think there were shadows, but the darkness didn't keep the Star from lighting up the sky. It didn't keep the Innkeeper from providing a safe place for the Baby to be born. Light from heaven and the singing of angels reassured the fearful shepherds. God was there.

All these years later when the Christmas season should lighten our hearts and brighten our lives, it is casting shadows instead. Why? Could it be that the preparation for the birthday celebration has become more important than the birth we celebrate? Could it be that elaborate giving has replaced personal gifts of time, and sharing, and giving of ourselves? Have the parties and entertaining left us with too little time or energy for worship? Have the things of the world become brighter than the *Light of the World*?

For more than fifty years we have set up the same small, handmade nativity scene under our Christmas tree. Through the years our children and grandchildren have played "First Christmas" with the now-worn figures. The best story that came from their play was a sad but true one. I passed by the crèche one day after the children had tired of playing with it and noticed that every one of the little wooden figures were inside the stable: shepherds, wise men, the donkey, the sheep, and the Holy Family. The only piece that was left on the outside was the baby Jesus. I couldn't help but think the display was a true portrayal of a modern-day Christmas celebration. Christ was left out.

This year I am going to let the lights twinkling on my Christmas tree remind me to brighten the lives of those in the shadows with a visit, a call, or an invitation to dinner. I can provide a shopping trip for a mother without funds, or take a decorated tree to a shut-in. I can't spread my light as far as the star of Bethlehem, but I can brighten up a lot of corners. I can make sure there's room in my Inn for Jesus.

> *"In Him, there was life, and that life was the light of all people. The Light shines in the darkness, and the darkness has not overpowered it" (John 1:4-5).*

The View From Old

I had a bit of a scare on Christmas Eve sitting around the tree with all of our children and our grandchildren, a visiting dog, and our old cats. I have always heard that just before a person dies their whole life passes before their eyes. It happened to me.

It started with the Christmas tree, laden with ornaments from as far back as the first Christmas we were married, each with a story to tell, a reminder of someone, or something from years past. There are old and worn trinkets made by the little hands of children, now grown, and a few extravagant ones I pinched pennies to buy. Most of all I think it was the tall, fragrant tree itself, covered with so many twinkling lights that swept me back to my childhood when every year my aunt and uncle put up the most beautiful of all trees. I doubt they ever knew the lasting inspiration they with left me, and it occurred to me that I would never know what memories my children were now making.

Only one of our grandchildren is still young enough to sit in the floor and shake the gifts while begging for the opening to begin. Watching him, I momentarily relived that feeling of anticipation. It was the year my brothers and I begged our mother to let us open our gifts before Christmas day. Mother gave in, as she often did, and Christmas Day was spoiled. That was the Christmas I learned that "no" was sometimes the best answer. I have never been tempted to do that again.

Our first child was born during the Christmas season, and to make that event more memorable, she was also the first grandchild for each set of grandparents. That was the year I truly connected with Mary, the Mother of Jesus. It was while I was reliving that special Christmas that one of our grandsons and his glowing wife announced that their gift to us this year was to be our first great-grandchild.

With all the families gathered in one place to exchanges gifts, presents were stacked on top of presents. Just having a gift for everyone wasn't enough for me; I wanted each of my gifts to match the person. I thought homemade gifts were the ultimate gifts, even though that often required staying up very late at night and sometimes experiencing disappointment when I missed the mark. That night I was asking myself the same questions as always. "Would everyone be happy with his or her gift? Was everyone treated reasonably the same? Would anyone be disappointed? Would everything fit? Who had overspent? What bills had gone unpaid in order to buy that special something so important to someone? Did our children spend money they couldn't spare to buy us gifts we didn't need?"

Choosing gifts for the grandchildren had become more and more difficult each year. How was I to know what to buy when I didn't even understand their new technical language? How was I to choose the right one when I didn't even know what "it" was? That was before the Lord created gift cards, which was exactly what they wanted all the time. Now all I have to do is add a personal note to their gift card, sit back, and watch them smile.

Recently a friend and I talked about how subtle God can be when He is dealing with us older folks. For instance, about the time we started getting lines and wrinkles in our face, our vision dimmed. When our accomplishments began to dwindle, our children began to achieve. When our physical strength declined, so did our ambition. Just when things got to be too complicated for us, our interests changed. Best of all, I have changed. From my present perspective, I have a very different concept of what is important and what isn't. I'd like to share that realization with my children, but time must be their teacher.

And so the evening passed with my life on re-run. I watched and listened to all that was going on around me. As scene after familiar scene was acted out, I could see my children and grandchildren now living for the first time in the different stages of life I had already passed through. It all came together to remind me of something I already knew. Each stage of my life has been the best.

I used to feel sad when I watched someone growing older, but this Christmas Eve as I traveled through time, I decided I was wrong. I loved being where I was in time. God does all things right! To paraphrase a scripture, *"Raise a child up in the way he should go and when you are old, you will be glad you did" (Proverbs 22:6).*

The View From Old

Dear. Santa Claus
  On behalf of your jenrouse Gratatude to deliver preasnents I would like you to have these cookies and Milk, I hope you enjoy them with pleasure, By the Way Could you get prancer to sign his pawprint?

Sincerly,
Anna Porter

Prancer's Pawprint